Mastering Mindful Leadership

105 Ways to Become the Leader
Your Employees Need You to Be

Johnny Russo

Manor House

Library and Archives Canada Cataloguing in Publication

Title: Mastering mindful leadership : 105 ways to become the leader your employees need you to be / Johnny Russo.
Names: Russo, Johnny (Writer on leadership), author.
Identifiers: Canadiana 20220428441 |
ISBN 9781988058856 (hardcover) |
ISBN 9781988058849 (softcover)
Subjects: LCSH: Leadership. | LCSH: Employee motivation. | LCSH: Motivation (Psychology) | LCSH: Success in business.
Classification: LCC HD57.7 .R87 2022 |
DDC 658.4/092—dc23

Cover art: Lightspring / Shutterstock / (Leadership and education symbol of human head with gears and cogs representing concept of sharing knowledge, thoughts).

First Edition
Cover Design-layout / Interior- layout: Michael Davie
192 pages / 29,683 words.   All rights reserved.
Published October 2022   / Copyright 2022
Manor House Publishing Inc.
452 Cottingham Crescent, Ancaster, ON, L9G 3V6
www.manor-house-publishing.com   (905) 648-4797

This project has been made possible [in part] by the Government of Canada. « *Ce projet a été rendu possible [en partie] grâce au gouvernement du Canada.*

Funded by the Government of Canada
Financé par le gouvernement du Canada

Canada

This book is dedicated to my two children, Luca and Siena. Being a dad is the greatest leadership journey in the world and I have learned much from being a dad that I pour into human-centred leadership. It is also dedicated to my entire family (thank you especially to my Mom and Dad for moulding me into the person I am today!), to the wonderful team members I have had over the years, and to the great leaders who have mentored me.

Foreword

Mastering Mindful Leadership will help you take your leadership expertise to a whole new level – leading to more motivated employees and increased business success and profitability.

Author Johnny Russo is at the forefront of the new age of enlightened leaders, who propel empowered loyal employees to achieve ever greater degrees of value, truly becoming a key catalyst for a company's success.

A seasoned business leader, Russo has managed countless teams over the course of a career that has harnessed the concept of mindful leadership to the success of the people he has been privileged to lead at an array of successful companies large and small.

Russo shares his considerable expertise in this breakthrough book, presenting key advice in 105 clear, short, easy-to-follow nuggets of wisdom that are pure gold for any leader striving for greater short term and long term success. His book will help you level up your leadership, no matter what level you're currently at.

This is the book you need to truly master mindful leadership and catapult yourself, your employees and everyone you come in contact with toward new and greater degrees of sustainable prosperity.

- **Michael B. Davie**, author, *Winning Ways*

Introduction

This is a book about a new wave of leadership, one that examines what it takes to manage a team of individuals to get them to buy into a team concept, to help inspire them, to motivate them, to get them to care about others, and to do it with respect and a smile on your face and theirs.

Leadership has changed. While leadership will always come in many shapes and sizes, the days of yelling to get your point across, ruling with a stern fist, controlling your people, playing punishing mind games with them, focusing on the negative and never accentuating the positive, and letting fear be your main leadership characteristic... those days are quickly becoming a thing of the past.

They are being replaced by a human-centric care for people, one which respects and values people and the organization, and one that drives results the right way. It's an approach to leadership where your people are just as important, and in many ways, *more* important, than profits. If you want to grow a sustainable business, you will need people who care about you and your business. And they can't genuinely care if your organization is run by fear.

This book has 105 traits. They are actionable and bite-sized. Why 105, you might ask? Well, theoretically, you can action two of these traits each week and become the leader you want to be in one year — the leader the world needs you to be. Or, you can work on one a week and follow a two-year plan to become the leader you know will drive success for yourself, as well as your team and your company. Or you may already be exhibiting many of these behaviours, in which case you can pick and choose which ones you want to work on.

While this book may cater to up-and-coming managers, or those new to managing a team at a company, a non-profit, government organization, or a sports team, many seasoned leaders and executives can take just as much from these impactful ways to lead. These traits may serve as reminders of the things we as leaders need to do more consciously and consistently. It's also great to share this book with your team, whether they aim to be in a management position or not.

I wrote this book because I have been motivated to be the leader I am by some great leaders who showed me what it is to be a great human being, and what it means to care for your people; I've also benefited from some great team members and colleagues, and some amazing authors whose words inspired me to lead in a better way, to help make people better, and not just focus on profits. Profits are hugely important, but they can't be our only driving motivator. We shouldn't prioritize profits *over* people; we should prioritize people *and* profits, with purpose. It's the only way forward.

I've added some blank pages as a Notes section at the end of the book in case you want to jot down some key points. I wish you luck on your leadership journey. My main advice is to keep learning, listening, caring, and empowering.

- Johnny Russo

Table Of Contents

"Do not follow where the path may lead. Go instead where there is no path and leave a trail."

—Ralph Waldo Emerson

1. Walk the Talk

Fail fast. Make mistakes. Adapt or die. You hear these calls to arms so often, it's almost fluff now. But Ray Dalio probably puts it best in his book, *Principles: Life and Work* (p.348):

> "Create a culture in which it is okay to make mistakes and unacceptable not to learn from them."[i]

Amen.

And live and abide by this, whether it's as an employee, boss, company or even sports team. You need to allow your employees room to grow and fail. But they must learn from mistakes. There must be a certain tolerance and acceptance for mistakes, big and small, but the successful employees will learn from them, and not keep making the same ones.

I remember when I was first starting out as a manager and I needed to fill a position rather quickly. We settled on someone who interviewed phenomenally well, but both my boss and I had a funny feeling about this person. We didn't feel like it was a cultural fit, but at the same time, this candidate was saying all the right things. Somehow, their words weren't coming off as authentic. It was almost as though this individual had read three or four books and was just reciting information from them back to us. Anyhow, we needed to fill the role, so we hired this individual.

They proceeded to show up late or miss meetings, they were disrespectful to others, and the cherry on top was that they once put an autoreply message on their email saying: "I'm busy from 10 a.m. to 2:00 p.m. answering emails, so please note I will not be available during this time." Needless to say, they were gone within three months. At least we fired (i.e., failed) fast. But I'll always remember to wait for the right person, rather than hiring someone my gut tells me is not the right fit. But if you hire fast, also be sure to fire fast. It was a big learning for me.

So, the next time you or your employee fails, do a quick deep dive and self-reflect on how you or they learned from it, and what they can do differently the next time.

2. Is Saying "Good Morning" So Hard?

I'm fascinated by people. Even more than that — especially since I started my career — I like to watch body language to see how people carry themselves. I look at their style, their posture, how they communicate when things go well, how they communicate in tougher times, and so on.

There is one habit I dislike, a lot. So many leaders, managers, and employees don't say "hello" or "good morning" at the start of the day. I have an issue with that. These simple words can make someone's day. They can make a team less defensive on a Monday morning. And they can send a jolt of serotonin into the brain.

Now, I know not everyone's a morning person, and it's hard to be happy every day of the week. And I'm not saying to strike up a full conversation before you've had your double mochaccino. But saying hello is not only common courtesy, it's respectful, and it makes the other person feel good.

And I'm not even advocating you go out of your way to say good morning to every co-worker, every day. What I'm advocating for, as a first step, is to say good morning to your team, your boss, those near your office or desk, the administrative team, or those you run into on your office coffee run.

Still on the fence?

Here Are Some Reasons You Should Say Hello in the Morning:

- It increases positive energy

- It can help you make a friend, or at the very least, get to know someone, as it could spark further conversation

- You'll be perceived as positive, and that is huge

- We're living in an altruistic society (you can challenge me on that, but I've never heard so many people talking about purpose and value as people today do), so saying good morning to someone could make their day, and it will likely make them smile and feel welcomed and appreciated

- Smiling is contagious—usually when you say hello, you will naturally smile, and others will likely smile right back at you. Try it!

- Saying hello can help others help you: at one point, the person you've been saying hello to for the last three months will help you on a project. And maybe they'll work a little extra because you're such a positive and nice person

Curmudgeons be damned. Let's all say it together: Good Morning.

3. The Waiting Game

Sometimes, you and your team patiently play the waiting game—waiting for other departments to send you things you need from them. But that's how bottlenecks start. Every company has them. Some tolerate them more than others. Your boss does not pay you to be patient. This isn't about stepping on toes, or not being conscious of sensitivities or politics. This is about driving results and doing what you get paid to do.

If you find yourself waiting one-to-two weeks—or more—for responses to emails, updates on projects, or requests you've made for access to a project or system, that's too long. But listen closely: go see the bottleneck in person, if possible (if you are working remotely, do it via Zoom, Teams, or some other video conferencing tool).

Imagine if you have five-to-ten bottlenecks (which are usually people or processes, sometimes both) and you eliminate half of them? Firstly, you'd be driving change in your company or department by not tolerating the waiting game. Secondly, you'd be actioning rather than waiting. Your boss, and your boss's boss, will notice. Also, you will *feel* a lot more valuable.

Take the first step. Send an invitation to meet with the person responsible for the approval or response you're waiting for on the project that means the most to you and meet with that person by the end of this week. I bet it helps.

4. Short Meetings

Are all your meetings 30 minutes or 60 minutes? Are some two-plus hours? Who is Outlook—or any other meeting calendar—to decide your meeting times because of their default settings?

Most 60-minute meetings can be completed in 45 minutes, saving you and all the other participants in the meeting 15 productive minutes in their day. The same goes for 30-minute meetings. If you shave unproductive minutes off everyone's calendar, think about how much more productive that will make people. They will also be less stressed. You can be the change agent in this. Today, instead of sending someone an invitation for a 30-minute meeting, send them an invite for 25 minutes, or 15 minutes. Some caveats:

1. Send an agenda *with* the meeting invite.

2. If others need to prepare something for the meeting, give them advance notice of at least a week.

3. Make sure everyone, including yourself, arrives or dials-in on time. A timely start to the meeting is critical for shorter meetings.

4. Dispense with pleasantries at the start of the meeting. The "how was your weekend" conversations can take place after the meeting in the hallway or chat room.

5. Send a recap after the meeting has ended and ensure accountability (with names) is in the follow up if something needs to be completed by attendees.

The business world needs people working more (on actual work) and meeting less (when those meetings aren't productive). Take the lead. Start scheduling 15- or 45-minute meetings; at some point, it'll become part of the company culture.

5. Change it Up

When you feel things are stagnating, taking too long to get done, or not being done well enough for your standards, change it up.

If you don't have a daily stand-up huddle, then add one. If you have one, add a second 15-minute meeting until the project you are working on is done.

If the project is simply not progressing, communicate more, not less, with your team. Usually, a project does not progress as quickly as you'd like because something or someone is unclear, perhaps concerning your expectations, or particular processes.

Make things simpler by overcommunicating, possibly simplifying the instructions and making sure to document changes or wants. All of this will go a long way to getting the project back on track.

6. Working More Is Often Not the Answer

Sometimes working more is not better.

If the team is working more than usual, either your demands are unreasonable, or, more likely, there is a broken process.

Oftentimes, things are taking too long because a process is not as streamlined as it could be, or you are using legacy technology and an extremely manual workflow, or perhaps employees are not clear on expectations.

The employees also might just be poor at managing their time. If an employee continues to overwork themselves for the sake of the team, they may burn out, causing you to backslide.

Step back, fix the broken process, create the automation, or help people be better at prioritizing.

The time you take to pause the project and address the issue will be worth it, as you'll have a healthy and motivated (and thankful) employee (or team).

7. Mondays and Tuesdays

On Sunday night, make a list and review all you need to do for the upcoming week, on a Monday-to-Friday plan (or include the weekend if need be, so Monday to Sunday). That's the first thing.

The second task may be painful. And while it may be painful at first, it will pay off by mid-week. Complete as much as 70% of your tasks on Monday and Tuesday. I know it's a big ask. But hear me out.

If you have 20-30 items on your to-do list, and you knock off 60%-70% of them on Monday and Tuesday you will have much more strategic planning or thinking time available for the latter half of the week. Yes, you may have to work extra hours, stay up late, watch less TV, or cut your lunch in half to do so much in these first two days, but it will be worth it. You will have more time for urgent items that may come up, and/or have more free time to spend with your team members.

The other trick is to complete your to-do tasks in order of priority, starting with the absolute most important item. So, if by the end of the week item Numbers 16-20 don't get done, they fall into the next week. Feel free to add personal chores or other non-work items to these lists.

Either way, if you have a structured approach to doing this, the rest of your week, from Wednesday to Friday (or Wednesday to Sunday, for some) will be achieved with more purpose, productivity, clarity, and satisfaction.

8. Create Your 1-2 Year Life Plan

Everyone has goals and timelines.

Some of those goals may be practical, far-reaching, or never-attain-but-die-trying goals.

But a goal without a plan is just a dream.

One way to come closer and closer to your personal and professional goals is to create a 1–2-year life plan. Think about it as large steps (design it that way too), with the following intervals:

> Six months
> One year
> One year and six months and
> Two years.

(Some people may find it's easier to draw their goals, so feel free to do that, too).

You can stop at one year if you find two years is too long, or you can even extend it further to three years if you think two years is too short a time period, but whichever you choose, make sure to input all the small and big goals you have in *both* your personal and professional life.

To get you going, here are some ideas for goals:

- Go on a Yoga retreat

- Meditate three times weekly

- Visit Cabo

- Get an MBA

- Change jobs

- Buy a house

- Learn new Excel skills

- Become a top chef

- Take your kids to Tuscany (okay, maybe that's mine) and

- Take French lessons

For what it's worth I find this works best when you intertwine your personal and professional lives.

9. Managing During Storms

The tough days and weeks are the ones where good and great managers distinguish themselves, where good and great leaders are born.

Don't pull away when your team needs you most. If there is a crisis, as tough as it may be to face it head-on and keep communicating with your team, this is when you are needed the most. Don't fear these situations — welcome them, embrace them, and manage forward. Don't hide and seek cover.

True leaders are born during the tough times. It's easy to manage during the easy times, just like it's easier to play in an exhibition game than a championship final, when the pressure goes up and the competition is fierce.

Manage bravely and over-communicate during tougher times. If you need a break, take one during the "easy" times when everything is going swimmingly.

10. The Ties That Bind You

In *Principles*, Ray Dalio, states something magical:

> *"Don't let the little things divide you when your agreement on the big things should bind you."[ii]*

Focus, and see the big picture. Petty things can crush you; big thinking can motivate you. (As an aside, think of any successful marriage or personal relationship. Do these words not ring true?)

Another note of caution: don't let negative gossip and pettiness pervade your team. When that starts to happen, talk to the various employee or parties involved, and try to end it there. Review the goals with them again, and make sure they understand they are here to achieve them, not gossip for hours on end.

11. Break The Tension

Every team faces it. Yet many managers cringe at the thought of tension.

But you will face tension amongst your team members. It's natural, especially as your team gets bigger. Today may be that day.

Here's what you do: book the late afternoon off with your team. Put a "hold" in their calendars. And then go out for a team building/bonding activity. Maybe an escape room, or axe throwing, or ping pong — whatever it may be, this is often the best time to do it. Have some fun, and then go for drinks and appetizers.

The next day, huddle up in the morning, talk about the fun, and get on with your day. The tension will be broken.

12. Check in With Former Colleagues

First of all, you should always care about your former team or colleagues you've worked with in the past, or even former vendors.

So, check in with these VIPs from time to time. See how they're doing. How's their family? How's their work life? How's their workout routine coming along? What book are they currently reading?

Secondly, you need to be constantly on the lookout for talent and good partners, so never stop checking in. You want them to remember you as someone who cared, even when you didn't work together. This goes a long way towards having people *want* to work with you, or for you, again.

Try and touch base with a former team member or former vendor at least once per month.

13. Recurring Meetings

If recurring meetings make you and the team or the other people in the meeting more productive, if they're helpful, and if you enjoy them, then by all means keep them going.

But if you have more than a 12-week recurrence on meetings, and they are a time-suck and not productive, kill them. If your boss has set them, talk to him/her. If your boss's boss has set them, it might be tough to cancel. If someone other than those two people has set them, then your boss needs to help you get out of them, pronto.

Bad meetings are a time-suck and a money-drain for companies, yet many companies keep them going. Be the change agent, and don't tolerate meetings that waste your time. And if you feel they are a waste, and your time can be better served, I assume the others in that meeting might feel the same but may be too afraid to challenge it.

Here's a question to ask the person setting up these meetings if you are feeling you are in too many of them with little value: "What are you expecting from this meeting or call?"

The response to that question will either help you understand why you are in these meetings and if they create value, or you'll get clarity that you were right, and it's a time-suck that needs to end now.

14. Defining What Being a Leader is

What is the definition of a leader? What does being a leader mean? I love this definition from John Quincy Adams:

> *"If your actions inspire others to dream more, learn more, do more and become more, you are a leader."*

Your team is filled with people with different personalities. And they each respond differently to various stimuli. The quicker you find what that is, and how they want to learn and grow, the quicker you can help, and truly lead them.

Kicking them while they're down is not one of those ways.

I've seen it too often: a tough stretch of mistakes in a peak period causes some leaders to change how they act. When things are going awry, sometimes that's when you need to be the most patient, and that's when your team members need your moral support and confidence.

There is an even deeper meaning of what leadership can mean, and the importance of being a leader who helps your team, especially when they need it most.

A beautiful poem called "Footprints in the Sand" that is largely attributed to Margaret Fishback (although several other people also claim to have written the poem), says:

"Lord, you said once I decided to follow you,
You'd walk with me all the way.
But I noticed that during the saddest
and most troublesome times of my life,
there was only one set of footprints.
I don't understand why,
when I needed You the most, You would leave me."

He whispered, "My precious child, I love you
and will never leave you
Never, ever, during your trials and testings.
When you saw only one set of footprints,
It was then that I carried you."

Help your people be great people.

15. Keep At It and Be Enthusiastic

Winston Churchill said this about success:

> *"Success consists of going from failure to failure without loss of enthusiasm."*

Read that again. And maybe read it once a week. And maybe, read that to your team today. You will fail at times on your way to success. You surely stumbled the first time you ran, or the first time you rode a bike, or the first time you were assigned a major project at work. So, it's important to keep this in mind, both for you, and for your team. They will fail. They are human. But you can help them up when they need a hand, or when they need some positive words, like those words above, which Churchill embraced.

Whether you want to admit it or not, your team looks up to you. And they look to you for motivation, positivity, encouragement, inspiration, and energy.

There are days when things will fail, many mistakes will be made, you have sleepless nights because your kids kept you up, or you don't feel well. Fight through it. You are a leader now.

Leaders stand in front of the group, and not behind them. Don't lose your enthusiasm, because while they may not tell you, your team needs it!

Sometimes we win. And sometimes we learn. German Physicist Max Planck said:

"When you change the way you look at things, the things you look at change."

Perspective can be a huge competitive advantage when dealing with so-called failure.

Failure (or learning) is a part of the journey to success. Embrace that notion, and then fight through it.

16. An Important List of "Don'ts"

Here are some things Managers and Leaders need to keep in mind to *not* do. (By the way, some of my greatest learnings as a leader have come from seeing leaders do things the wrong way, and then doing the exact opposite).

- Don't be distant in times when your employees need to hear and see you. It's easy to hide; don't be the leader who does.

- Don't get used to mediocrity. If you and your team are providing average or subpar results, and it's been that way for a while, you need to change things up.

- Don't let your ego get in the way. Don't pretend you don't need help. You are not perfect. You are still learning. You may need to ask for help. Do so before any major escalation is needed. Your boss will understand and be thankful in the end. It also builds trust.

- Don't fear failure. Fear doing nothing about it. When you fail, work twice as hard to get back up and four times as hard to succeed.

17. Always Think About Tomorrow

You certainly need to have one eye on the present but remind yourself that great leaders are also looking forward. That skill—to look at the present and focus on the present to achieve your yearly goals, while your mind is constantly thinking about the future—is what separates the good from the great.

Wang Qishan, a high-ranking Chinese politician, and the current Vice Present of the People's Republic of China, once said:

"Unattainable goals appeal to heroes. Capable people are those who sit there worrying about the future. The unwise are those who worry about nothing."iii

Take an hour right now and map out what you think your industry looks like in one, three, five, 10, and 20 years. It will force you to think huge with no limits. Look forward, and you'll likely find a bright(er) future.

18. Being a Manager vs. a Leader

Do you ever wonder what separates a manager from a leader? When I was younger, at about age 15, I entered the workforce for the first time. I worked at a reception hall as a busboy, and then quickly became a waiter and even a bartender. Bartending at a wedding at an open bar can be insanely fun and nuts at the same time. At that age, I just worked. I didn't think about leadership or communication too much. But I did notice how the head waiters took charge.

As I moved into my first "real" full time job in marketing, I became more aware of human capital. I saw good and bad. I quickly set a goal to become a manager. I wanted to be "in charge" and have a team. Like many, I thought the title would give me respect. Five years later I became a manager and had a team of two. I was responsible for two people. And I took that seriously.

Little did I know I was learning the difference between being a manager and what it takes to lead people. It's not about a top-down approach. It's not about managing tasks. It's about being a captain for your team, during good times and bad. Helping them work through their challenges, allowing them to make mistakes, guiding them, and not simply telling them what to do. It's also about making sure to celebrate their wins and achievements, both big and small.

Some senior executives stay in the "manager" role for their entire career. Success may follow them, but are they fulfilled? Were their teams excited to come to work? If they left, would any employees follow them and want to work with them again?

In Kevin Cashman's inspiring leadership book, *Leadership from The Inside Out: Becoming a Leader for Life*, he quotes Paul Walsh, Chairman and CEO of Diageo, one of the world's largest producers of spirits and beers.

> "As managers, we are trained as cops, who are supposed to keep things under control. As leaders, we need to shift from control to trust. I don't care who you are or how great you are, no one person can totally claim victory or totally abstain from the defeat."[iv]

Cashman then put those comments into perspective, with a great summary:

> "Learning to move our belief from thinking, 'I have all the answers,' to 'together, we have all the answers,' is the first crucial step to Interpersonal Mastery."

Now, I'm not saying you can't be a leader with a "we'll do it my way" mentality. But as we head into a phase in leadership which will be more about inclusivity, positivity, collaboration, and values, you may want to adjust and adapt your leadership style(s) today.

Become a manager, and then grow into a leader. Much like the captain of a sports team, win or lose, he/she takes the pressure off his/her team members, he/she checks in with them, motivates them when they need some encouragement, and inspires them to be better. Be their captain, be their leader. The world needs leaders who truly care about their people.

19. The Three Phases of Life

In his book, *Principles*, Ray Dalio notes that these are the three phases of life:[v]

Phase 1: We're dependent on others, and we learn

Phase 2: Others depend on us, and we work.

Phase 3: Others no longer depend on us and we no longer have to work - we're free to savour life.

Sometimes work and life cross. Scratch that…they most likely always will. When you break it up into these phases, it may enlighten you, or scare you. But whichever phase you are currently in, be mindful of the impact you are having on other people. If you have a family or lead a team, then, as Phase 2 mentions, people are depending on you. Don't take that mission lightly.

To think of it another way: imagine your employee at the dinner table after work, talking to her husband about her day, and her boss. That boss is *you*. The next words out of her mouth will either be positive and respectful, or negative and disrespectful. But how you lead your team will determine the words she, and the rest of your team, will use.

Make it your mission to serve others. Make it your mission to inspire and empower your team.

20. The Importance of Goal Setting

How can you or your team crush goals if you don't have them?

Whether it's personal, professional, philanthropic, or any other type of goal, if you don't have them, you may be lacking direction.

Now, goals without a plan to achieve them are much like having a dream with no goals.

People who set goals are more successful and accomplish more than those who don't.

In the book, *The Success Principles: How to Get from Where You are to Where You Want to Be*, author Jack Canfield cites a number of studies, which suggest if you merely think about goals, you are 42% more successful than someone who does not.

But that success rate increases to 56% when you write down your goals, and 64% when you think about, write down, and share your goals with a friend.[vi]

That last point also speaks to accountability.

If you share your goals with your team, and they do the same, you will all be more accountable.

I like to always have three-to-five personal goals and three-to-five professional goals with deadlines spread out over the course of the next one-to-two years.

Preferably there's a mix of short-term and long-term goals on that list.

Now make sure you dive deeper than the surface for these goals, and make sure they are each measurable (*how much?*) and they each have a clear timeline (*by when?*).

Using the SMART goal framework is a good place to start: Make sure your goals are: Specific, Measurable, Relevant, Achievable and Time Bound.

So, get into the habit of goal setting, and then work on crushing those goals, and by doing so, you'll be helping your team perform to its maximum capability and creativity.

21. To-Do Lists

Don't roll your eyes – and don't dread To-Do Lists.

Much like meetings, which are often dreaded as a waste of time when there is no structure, if your to-dos don't get you closer to your goals for the day, week, month, or year, then yes, they too are useless.

But a precise, well-defined, well-coordinated to-do list makes you much more productive. Once your team sees this, you can teach them how to do it.

First, you need to set and plan your to-do list the night (or, even better, the week) before. Don't waste time during the current day planning your day. It will go awry.

Secondly, do the hard things first. Do the things that are the toughest, biggest, and require your most attention first. These are usually the to-dos that are major projects or have a major impact and you need to get them done. So do them.

Thirdly, the easy stuff will get completed if you plan well, so don't do the easy things first just to knock them off your list. (And if need be, these can always be completed the following day). And the next point really underscores the importance of this:

Fourthly, build a buffer or have a time block of 30 minutes (or longer) each day. There will always be a new last-minute addition to the list, or something your boss or your team needs, or a meeting you'll be pulled into that was not scheduled. So, build it in, and don't stress about it.

22. Show Trust in Your Employees

People talk about trusting their team all the time. They say: "of course I trust them." And then they micromanage the crap out of them, and tell them everything they need to do, down to the smallest detail. Raise your hand if you want a leader who really does not have trust or faith in you? Exactly. Sometimes, as a leader, you need to direct your people, and then get out of their way.

I had two super-talented employees on my team; one was a designer and the other worked on the brand side. We were re-purposing content another team needed for a presentation. I wanted the request to flow through these two team members, so they were involved from the start. When the time came, they asked if I wanted to see what they had done or if they could just send it on. I said "I have full faith that you two did a great job. Just send it." The reply came back: "We knew you trusted us, and figured you'd say that. Thanks for the confidence."

While working together for the last two years certainly helped, I knew their integrity and the quality of their work. I also know they didn't want to disappoint me. Why? Because I trusted them, and I showed it daily.

So, as leaders, we can't just talk a good game; actions speak so much louder than words. Show your team members you trust them. They'll never want to disappoint you.

23. Take the High Road

At some point in your leadership career, a colleague will be fired or let go for various reasons.

Sometimes, you will not have enjoyed working with this person. You may have even complained about them, to their face or otherwise. You may have had disagreements with them.

And you may not have even respected them as a professional. But if and when they do get fired, take the high road. Don't gloat, don't say "I told you so," don't say you "knew this would happen." Just acknowledge it by saying "that's too bad," if you wish (or just stay quiet), and that's the end of it.

If they were that bad a person to work with anyway, not giving it any attention will help the company get over the problem even sooner, proving this employee was indeed a distraction and a bad fit.

Be a good professional and take the high road at all times, especially when someone else loses their job.

24. It's Okay to Have a Bit of Fun

Companies today can often still be a bit stuffy and stuck up. Business is business, and work is work. But you can still smile, laugh, and have fun while you work—and with the colleagues you work with. It also starts with you. If you as a leader allow it, your team will embrace it. As long as (and this is important) the work is being done, milestones are met, goals are crushed, and results are being met or exceeded. But a happy team is usually a solid and productive one.

Companies need cultures that are more fun, so don't shy away from it. Also, please note that if you have a successful team, and are having fun along the way, other "stuffy" departments may be jealous. Be prepared for that—but be a change agent for fun.

25. Feedback Question May Change You

In his book *The Success Principles*, Jack Canfield writes about the most powerful question he learned from someone very successful, and he's passed it on to friends and readers:

> On a scale of 1 to 10, how would you rate the quality of our relationship (service or product) during the last week (two weeks/ month/quarter/year/semester/season)?[vii]

This can be re-purposed into almost anything you need feedback on: how would you rate the meeting we just had? How would you rate my speaking presentation? How would you rate this meal? How would you rate this book?

Any rating of less than a 10 then gets this follow up question: What would it take to make it a 10?

Powerful, powerful stuff. So, at your next Monday team meeting, or your next one-on-one with your employee(s) or boss, ask this feedback question, and ask it for any area you want to improve on. The feedback you get may be game-changing. Feedback is a gift. Make sure you are always open to receiving it. Granted, some feedback you may instinctively not want to action, and that's okay, but you should at least always listen to it with an open mind.

26. Do You Listen?

It's a pet peeve of mine when people continually cut people off when they are speaking, especially when they don't recognize or apologize for doing it. It's very disrespectful, regardless of what the person is saying. This is even more important when and if you are cutting off your team members.

God gave us two ears and one mouth. When others talk, listen attentively. Don't try and figure out what you will say next. Don't interject in the middle of their point to prove you know more. Don't look away from them when they are talking. Don't glance at your phone while they speak.

So, make sure you let people finish their sentences, and really listen and focus on what they are saying. A good little trick is to have them finish and pause for one-to-two seconds after their last word. Maybe neither of you like awkward silence, but the pause is effective, as it shows you are truly listening and soaking the info in, and it also makes the other person feel heard and as though they got the opportunity to get their point across.

As you may know, I'm a collector of motivational quotes and inspiration. And here is one I routinely check myself against, from Winston Churchill:

"Courage is what it takes to stand up and speak; courage is also what it takes to sit down and listen."

Being an effective leader starts with being an effective listener.

27. Will You Match the Salary?

At some point, one of your team members will quit for another opportunity or leave because they don't enjoy working at your company anymore.

And at some point, you will also get an employee who may be bluffing about having "another job" but wants you to match their fictitious salary anyway.

Whether they are bluffing or they want to leave even though they still enjoy working at your company, you have two choices:

1. If you value them, and they are an integral part of your team/company/culture, try to match or better the salary. If you have an MVP (Most Valuable Player), don't let that person become someone else's MVP.

2. If they are merely okay, call their bluff. But honestly, regardless of whether they are bluffing or looking for more money (that you won't give), it's only a matter of time before they leave anyhow. They'll likely be disengaged from this point onward. So strongly consider exiting them shortly after the real or fake bluff.

28. Do You Read?

One of my favourite questions to ask during a job interview is, "Do you read?" I always find it shows a willingness to keep on learning, especially after doing so much reading during your academic years.

Reading and learning are imperative to success. They are linked, so I try and gauge if my potential team member likes learning and is never satisfied with the status quo. I feel it is a good measure of an individual's potential value to my team.

You can also tell how truthful an employee is being. Because if they answer yes to that question, the next one should be "what book or blog are you currently reading?" Any hesitation may intimate that they are bending the truth.

As for my current team, I always want to know what they are currently reading. If they are not reading anything, or say they have "no time," I try to drop hints that they should be reading, before dropping the hammer... I place a book on their desk. Hint. Hint.

You should try it today. Send a member of your team the book that had the biggest impact on your career.

29. The Rule of 1, 5, and 10

Imagine doing one thing daily to continuously improve personally or professionally. For example, meditating one time per day for three minutes. That would be 365 days of meditation, or 1,095 minutes.

Imagine doing five things daily to continuously improve personally or professionally. For example, reading or writing five pages per day. That would be reading or writing 1,825 pages (or reading about seven average-length books) in one year.

Imagine doing 10 things daily to continuously improve personally or professionally. For example, biking 10 kilometres per day, or asking 10 mentors/celebrities/investors/book publishers to lunch, or drinking 10 glasses of water per day. That would be 3,650 kilometres biked in a year or asking 3,650 mentors/celebrities/investors/book publishers to lunch (one of them is bound to say yes!) or drinking 3,650 glasses of water in a year.

Granted, the 10x rule may be tough. But you would probably agree that the one and/or five is doable. Yes, it certainly is! Now, impart this to your team. Because if you want to get the most out of them, having them follow either the 1x, 5x, or 10x rule will multiply their contribution and development. And look in the mirror. You need to be on this plan, too. Level up your development.

30. Integrity a True Leadership Staple

Writer C.S. Lewis said it best:

"Integrity is doing the right thing, even when no one is watching."

As a leader, you need to make sure the line is not blurred between core values and driving success at any cost. If you are dishonest, your employees will also be dishonest.

If you don't tolerate mistakes, your employees will be afraid to speak up, thus covering things up, and lying. If you take all the credit for the team's success, the team will lose respect for your leadership.

The definition of integrity in its purest form is the quality of being an honest person and having strong moral principles. Don't blur the lines on these two critical life principles: honesty and ethics. Much like a child looks up to their parent and looks to them for guidance, your team does, too. We often forget that. Because they are mostly adults, we don't think of our team members as looking up to us or seeking our guidance. They do. Believe me. They absolutely do! So, show them the right way.

Without integrity, true leadership may be far away from your grasp.

31. Today May Be *the* Day

Out of nowhere, today may be the day one of your employees or colleagues vents, gets upset at you, or disrespects a team member. This will likely happen to you at some point.

Here's the best advice I can give: breathe. And then be empathetic.

If this is indeed not ordinary behaviour for this individual, it may be that he/she is having a bad day. Perhaps they are depressed, feeling anxious because of all the work they have to complete, or they have an unresolved personal issue at home.

Whatever it may be, try to be empathetic and understanding with them first. Listen, and then ask them if they are okay.

On the other hand, if they do this regularly, today may be the day to let them go.

32. Hi, First Name

Don't let your first email to your team members in the morning—especially on a Monday—start with:
> "Can you…?" or

> "Here's what I need…" or

> "Call me."

Remember to always be courteous and respectful. The employee on the receiving end will be way more receptive if you start with, "Hi Nico. How was your weekend? Can you get me this report for end of day? Thanks."

Or how about, "Hey Katrina, hope you had a great night and caught up on all the reading you wanted to do. On today's to-do's, here's what I need from you: call the agency, get the digital ad spend report, and look out for a meeting invite from our VP."

Or something like "Hey James. Didn't want to bother you last night. But can you call me this morning so we can align on the presentation taking place on Friday? Thanks James."

Saying hi, using people's first names, and asking about their previous day, night, or weekend goes a long way towards not making your employees feel anxious or stressed when you ask them for something.

33. Show Passion

Whatever your role or position is, if you are entrusted to lead, your employees are looking for someone to follow. And they want to trust you. To believe in you. And have confidence in you. But they also want someone who feels passionate about the mission and values behind what your company or organization stands for.

So, rather than reading through your plan in a monotone fashion, make sure to be lively, engaged with your team (eye contact is huge), and show you love this topic/plan/product/challenge, etc. If whatever you are planning for or presenting comes off as ho-hum with a "geez, not another challenge" attitude, then your team won't want you at the helm. Show passion. It's a good thing.

One of my favourite quotes on this subject comes from American poet and essayist Ralph Waldo Emerson, who said:

"Enthusiasm is one of the most powerful engines of success. When you do a thing, do it with all your might. Put your whole soul into it. Stamp it with your own personality. Be active, be energetic, be enthusiastic and faithful, and you will accomplish your object. Nothing great was ever achieved without enthusiasm."

If that doesn't make your spine tingle, you are likely not passionate about what you do or want to do in life. Find your passion, and enrich others with it.

34. Gifting

Whatever policy or culture you want to create as a leader, when it comes to gifting, just make it consistent. So, if you go out for lunch as a team for everyone's birthday, make sure you don't skip anyone.

If you buy Starbucks gift cards on everyone's birthday as their gift, make sure you do it for everyone. I'm not saying the amounts can't be a little different—maybe you give more to your director, or someone who did some extra heavy lifting in the last quarter—but make sure you don't miss an employee on their birthday.

(Note on that: send a calendar invite to yourself at least one week before their birthday and send another invite to yourself for 8:00 a.m. on the employee's birthday so you don't forget). And this goes for Christmas gifts, or Valentine's Day cards, or thank you notes. Try to be fair.

The point is, just be consistent. Your entire team will appreciate it.

35. Throw Them a Bone

If you're team has delivered on a huge project, or been delivering consistently for a few months, maybe today's the Friday where you have them all finish early or take the team out for a meal and some drinks. If you're all working virtually, send your team a meal via Uber Eats.

You need to celebrate your wins and the hard work, and the *unexpected* times you celebrate will have a huge positive impact on team morale.

36. Trust and Working from Home

Working from home is always a hot topic. But during the COVID-19 pandemic in 2020 and beyond, this became every company's burning topic. We also saw a lot of companies put the onus on employees to decide if they wanted to continue to work from home permanently. Many technology companies already had these policies in place. But success with these practices comes down to trust, regardless of whether you're a hip new start-up or a traditional company.

Do you trust your employees? If the answer is not a resounding "YES!" then why did you hire them? Okay, maybe that's harsh since you wanted to trust them when you hired them. But at least grant me this: if you hired them, and then found out you could not trust them, why keep them around? If they failed in a face-to-face environment when you and their team members were around, how do you think they'll fare working from home? You know the answer.

So, if you trust your employees or team members, and this goes from the CEO on down to junior-level positions, then provide the option to work from home. If you don't trust them, why keep them around? Employees crave flexibility today more than ever. Top talent will demand it. So, companies should be proactive about it.

37. Stand Up for What You Believe In

If you believe in something, you need to stand up for it. If you believe in your strategy—and see no other option—yet your organization wants to continue with the status quo, which you know is bleeding the company into irrelevance, do you really want to stay? How will you face your team if you don't believe in what you are committing to? Don't sign them up because you became a yes man/ma'am along the way.

Now, this is different from having a united front as an executive or management team. You often need to do that. What I'm talking about here is your own business unit's strategy.

All I'm saying is don't go along with a plan you know will fail. Try to change it or ask if this is the right place for you and your leadership abilities. Your team wants to follow a true leader, not a fake yes-man or yes-woman. If your company hired you to deliver a strategy, and in your heart, you had the perfect one, but senior leaders have changed it so much that it's not yours anymore, pay close attention to how willing they actually are to adapt.

Stand up for what you believe in. Or consider your alternatives.

38. Parkinson's Law: Pursuit of Progress

Get really, really, good at estimating how long tasks and projects take to complete very well (maybe not perfect, but very well).

If you get good at estimating, and help your team to do the same, then you can get really good at pushing out more projects from them (output) and accomplishing more (action).

> *"Work expands to fill the time available for its completion."*

So said a man named Cyril Northcote Parkinson, and it has become known as Parkinson's Law: The Pursuit of Progress.

If you *think* a project will take three years to complete, it likely will take as long, or longer. But what if you could get that project done sooner? What if it took two years? What if you truly focused on and believed it could take two years to complete, shaving off one entire year? That would mean you had an extra 365 days to complete other work.

Let me ask you this: if I said you had to write a 20-page biography of your life, and you had seven days to do so, how long would it take you? After some procrastination and self-reflection, you'd likely take six-to-seven days to complete it. But what if I told you that you had to submit it in less than 24 hours? My guess is you would get it done, and it would come from the heart and likely be even better than the one, which took you a week to complete.

So, be realistic on timelines but know that the better you get at planning your time, the more effective your team gets and, likely, the quality of work gets even better too! Make time work for you.

39. Create More Leaders

"The most essential work of the leader is to create more leaders."

Those are the words of Mary Parker-Follett, a social worker and pioneer in organizational theory and behaviour. Today or tomorrow is the day you set aside a time block. Take two or three hours—or half a day if you can—and plan a succession plan for your team. Plan their development. Plan their areas of improvement (things to work on). Outline their strengths (things to continue doing well). Work on their blindspots.

If Jimmy wants to be a manager in two years, help him get there. Chart his growth plan. If Chelsea wants to move from Customer Service Coordinator to Social Media Specialist, list the things she needs to do to make that happen, including the education and work she needs to make that change. If Paul needs to be better at managing up, give him the formula to do so. And if you don't know what some of your team members want next, or you don't know where they slot in, have an open and honest discussion with them on their short- and mid-term goals and future.

Help your company and your team by creating more leaders—future leaders your company and your industry need.

40. The Six Questions

It's important to hold yourself accountable. In his book *Triggers: Creating Behavior That Lasts— Becoming the Person You Want to Be,* renowned executive coach Marshall Goldsmith outlines six ways you can help make sure you are a fantastic leader (and a good human being). The six questions he invites readers to ask are:

1. Did I do my best to set clear goals?
2. Did I do my best to make progress toward my goals?
3. Did I do my best to find meaning?
4. Did I do my best to be happy?
5. Did I do my best to build positive relationships?
6. Did I do my best to be fully engaged?

If you can ask yourself these questions on a weekly—or monthly—basis, you will not only become good at leading people, but you will also become a good person. They are both crucial elements to obtain and maintain on your lifelong leadership journey. Being a great leader and being a great human being go hand in hand. Don't let anyone tell you differently. Now, that may have looked different 30 or 40 years ago, but these days, both are linked. Would you want to work for a leader who was not a good human being? I don't think so.

41. The What and the Why

Why are you doing what you do? Have you defined it? Why do you want to be a great leader? You've picked up this book because you obviously want to be a great leader and improve your leadership abilities. But why? Let's help you define that:

- This exercise will take anywhere from 15-30 minutes, so make sure you're in a place with as little distraction as possible

- This exercise will help you create your life intention matrix (why do you want to do what you do) and also start you on your dream builder process. Dream away and chip away at your goals to get all you ever wanted.

- I have been using *Life Purpose Playbook: The Ultimate Guide to Goal Setting and Daily Planning* by Judy Machado-Duque as my daily planning, goal setting, and purpose building tool since 2018. It is the best one I have found. Feel free to use others, but I highly recommend Judy's playbook. You can find it on Amazon or check out her site at: www.lifepurposeplaybook.com.

- These specific exercises can be found on Pages 14, 15, and 17 (version 1.1 of Judy's playbook)[viii]

MY LIFE INTENTION MATRIX ™

Now that you have clarified your purpose, you can create a clear LIFE INTENTION.

This concept is similar to a mission statement, a one or two sentence statement describing the reason you exist. But it is written as an INTENTION. This will provide clarity and give you a sense of purpose. It gives you permission to say NO to things that are distractions. Your LIFE INTENTION may change over time, as you acquire more life experiences and skills.

What is your LIFE INTENTION? What can you do with your life to become fulfilled, to create value for others, to help the greater good of humanity?

The more you clarify what it is you want, the more you will be able to make decisions about priorities in your life. You may then start to attract people, opportunities, circumstances and events into your life to make it happen.

Your LIFE INTENTION should be easily said by you and should be **RECOGNIZABLY YOURS.**

STEP 1

Circle 1-4 ACTION words within the SPACE below.
Choose words that most resonate and inspire you! Feel free to add any others.

Accomplish

Express Master Acquire Connect Measure

Construct Facilitate Restore Administrate Adopt

Co-ordinate Foster Motivate Safeguard Counsel Advise

Create Gather Negotiate Save Affect Generate Nurture Sell

Defend Give Serve Organize Share Deliver Guide Analyze

Demonstrate Heal Appreciate Help Perform Spread Assist

Discover Host Play Support Practice Believe Distribute Illuminate

Implement Prepare Dream Improve Present Build Drive Produce

Teach Educate Inform Progress Team Cause Inspire Touch Change

Embrace Integrate Promote Empower Translate Encourage

Pursue Travel Engage Collect Engineer Reclaim Enhance

Coach Launch Reduce Enlighten Lead Refine Validate

Communicate Enlist Learn Reflect Value Enliven

Light Volunteer Entertain Love Write

Evaluate Release Manage Explore

Manifest

STEP 2

In the SPACE below, write WHAT services you would like to be offering in life.

For example:
coach, engineer, create systems, public speaking, workshops

STEP 3

In the SPACE below, write to WHOM you would like to offer your services.

For example:
children, businesses, entrepreneurs, animals or people in general.

STEP 4

Transfer the ACTION words you selected from STEP 1 into this SPACE above. This becomes the VALUE you create for others in your life.

For example:
promote, empower, entertain, enlighten, alive

STEP 5

In this SPACE above, transfer any of YOUR TOP 5 VALUES (page 13) that align with your purpose.

For example:
time freedom, balance

STEP 6

In the SPACE below, combine STEPS 2, 3, 4 and 5 to complete **YOUR** LIFE INTENTION.

Here is an example.... My LIFE INTENTION is to empower entrepreneurs, to create balance and become enlightened & alive through interactive workshops.

You did it! Congratulations!

LIVE EVERY DAY WITH **INTENTION** AND WATCH YOUR LIFE TRANSFORM!

MY LIFE INTENTION MATRIX

If you don't know where you are going, you will end up exactly there! Now that you have a clear LIFE INTENTION, It's time to get specific on all your DREAMS.

In this exercise, you will write your goals starting with the words I AM (then write your goal). This will create BELIEF in the present moment so that you BECOME THE GOAL.

For example:
"I AM spending my days working from my modern home office as a journalist, creating value for others".
"I HAVE an abundant & generous mindset".

These I AM or I HAVE statements become a command to the Universe to create instant belief and results.

This activity will help you to BELIEVE it before you see it. It will create the possibility for you that your DREAMS can become reality.

Take a deep breath. On the SPACE below, write down all of your DREAMS, big and small. Here are some questions you can use to help spark your imagination:

• Where is your DREAM home and what EXACTLY does it look like? Why do you want this home?
• Describe the way you spend your DREAM days?
• If you didn't have to work to earn money, what would you do?
• How would you LOVE to contribute to the world?
• What is everything you wish to BE, DO and HAVE in your life?

Don't stop writing until you fill this page! Write as fast as you can. Keep moving your pen & stay inspired. MAGIC happens when you write down your DREAMS.

MY DREAM BUILDER™

17

66

Now that you have defined your own why and life intention, it's time to ask if your company has defined it. If you own your own company, you need to figure this out.

If you are a consultant or run an agency, you need this front and centre. If you are a cog in the bigger machine, send a note to your boss, your boss's boss, and all the way to the top if you have to: your company needs a "why."

And you can always help define it, regardless of your title, hierarchy, gender, age, or experience.

At the very least, your own "why" will act as your personal compass. And that is certain to lead you in the right direction.

42. Don't Avoid Uncomfortable Situations

Are you too nice for the betterment of your team? I'll come right out and say it: do you avoid uncomfortable situations and tolerate mediocre work because you don't want to hurt anyone's feelings? Many leaders at the beginning of their careers—and even seasoned leadership veterans—do this, so don't worry – you're not alone. And I can help fix this.

Step 1: Know the more you give respectful, critical feedback, the easier it gets.

Step 2: Most employees will realize you are likely right, and embrace that feedback, even if they sulk for a day or two.

Step 3: If you have employees who don't embrace any type of feedback, are these the type of team members you want to build around, or with? Unlikely.

Step 4: In the next six months, keep track of how many times you've given feedback. If it's less than three times—meaning only once every two months—you're likely still too afraid to give feedback. If you're between six and ten, you're doing great. If you've had these conversations more than 10 times in the last six months, you're well on your way to becoming a super, highly communicative leader.

43. Not allowed to Fix Broken System? Leave

Are you at a company where you feel the processes are broken? I'm pretty sure you're nodding your head yes. Maybe some of you just screamed it. Yes!

Now for the more important question: Are you at a company where you feel processes—or strategy, or culture, or something else—is broken, and you've been brought in to fix it, but after one year, little progress has been made and that has you feeling like things won't change?

Said another way, is the system broken? Are profits declining? Is the business's purpose cloudy? Is culture sliding backwards? Is the company doing the same things it did 20 years ago?

Do you and everyone around you see the issues, but your boss or boss's boss won't "allow" you to fix it?

Bad news: they may never let you fix things.

If after a year of trying the company still doesn't change, it's because of one of two reasons:

Number 1.
Management doesn't have 100% trust and faith in your role or your abilities.

Or, the more likely reason...

Number 2.
They hate change and prefer to languish in a loss of profits than equip themselves for change.

Then you have to do some soul searching and decide: should you stick around and collect a paycheck, or go elsewhere for change?

44. Your Next Monday

On your next Monday, whether that's today, tomorrow, or next week, talk to your team members, but not about work.

Take 10 or 15 minutes for each member of your team, and don't talk about work. Ask about their weekend. Ask what they did. Did they read any good books over the weekend? Were the kids a handful? Did they get to exercise or try that restaurant they've been meaning to eat at?

Sometimes, it's important to *not* talk about work. You want to be a human leader. That means you care about results, yes. But you need to care about your people.

And your people will work their hearts out for a leader who cares about them. So be sure to consistently take the time to talk about them, and not about their work.

45. Personal Goal Setting

If you want to be the best leader you can be, you'd better have a list of goals you want to attain or achieve. I don't know many employees who want to follow a leader who doesn't have small and large goals, someone who is always wanting more and something better for themselves, someone who has loads of drive.

Now, here's what I want you to do:

Ask your team to list the top five or 10 things they want to do, accomplish, or achieve this year (or in the next 12 months). It could be travelling to Las Vegas for the first time, completing a certification they've been wanting to get, or reading one book a month.

Hopefully, they are comfortable sharing them with you. If they are not, that's okay. But if they are, schedule quarterly touch-bases with them to see their progress. Is there any way you can help push them to ignite their goal-setting achievement?

Lead them down the path to success. Anyone can set a goal. But goal crushers are the ones you want on your team — the ones that challenge themselves, stretch themselves, and reach with all their might for what they want. Help them be driven to achieve their goals.

46. Make Decisions More Easily

If you're managing a team, it means your staff members are likely sending you presentations that need review, emails that need comments, or designs and other collateral that need your feedback.

Put yourself in their shoes. Remember when you were just starting out and it was like pulling teeth to get responses to your emails from "that" manager? Don't be one of them!

There are likely two reasons for the lack of response, or prolonged silence:

1. You are afraid to make decisions.

2. You have poor time management skills.

But let's try and tackle both of those in one fell swoop: on each Friday before you head out for the weekend, flag each email (say with the colour blue) for items that need a follow up.

Also, create a meeting invite for Monday morning—just a hold, really—for any decisions that need to be made or presentations that need to be reviewed (literally paste them into your invitation), or add in the people you need to meet with if you need a higher-ranking approval for some of these items.

Also, if there is a delay in giving your team feedback, let them know about it.

When Monday comes, block out 15-20 minutes to review that calendar invite, and review all the items flagged in blue.

Don't make decision-making or feedback a hassle. You're in this position of "authority" for a reason. Remember, *you* teach your team what is acceptable and not acceptable. Is a lack of response something you want to be teaching? Not at all. So, try your best not to make it a habit.

47. Reading List Update

Great leaders read. It's no secret. Great leaders search out knowledge, they have a thirst for it. Ralph Waldo Emerson once said:

"The mind, once stretched by a new idea, never returns to its original dimensions."

That. Is. Gold.

Heed that advice. Never stop learning.

I know some people don't like books. Okay. Then delve into another form of learning, whether it's in-person or online courses, blogs, articles, audio books, podcasts—whatever it may be. Learning enriches you as a person and as an effective leader.

So, today, update or renew your reading list for the next two years. At the very least, this list should be for 24 books (one book per month).

I'm not saying you have to read one book every month, but if you have a long list at least you don't have to think about which books are next. You'll have an unranked list to choose from.

Even better, choose some books that make you well-rounded: have some on personal development, sports, the economy, a biography or two, health and fitness, and relationships. Or you can focus on one or two core categories—like health and personal development—and align your reading and learning to those topics for the next year or two.

Whatever way you choose to structure your list make sure you have some books—or podcasts—for each. That is a sure-fire way to become a well-rounded person who is constantly learning.

48. Stand Behind Your Words

Once, while I was on paternity leave, a senior director at the company where I worked criticized my team.

Her concern was that my team members seemed to be having fun while they worked. She reasoned that the fact my team didn't seem to be stressed meant they just didn't have enough work. Her foreign and old-school thinking dictated that people who smile, say hello, laugh, and enjoy work was that they either aren't doing much work, or simply don't have enough on their plates.

In her own world, she felt stressed, and she needed her team to be stressed. They felt her wrath. She didn't believe work was to be enjoyed, and she would criticize anyone who didn't follow those rules, including the members of my team.

Let me repeat that she spoke out about my team while I was on paternity leave and not present. When I returned and found out about this, she pulled me aside to give me an "I'm sorry, but really not" apology. Needless to say, she didn't have many fans and she was subsequently let go. An important point here is that when you need to say something critical about a party or person, try to make sure they're in the room, or talk to them right away.

77

Everyone makes mistakes in the heat of the moment, and a simple text or talk could have helped.

And if anyone tells you that you shouldn't smile and try to enjoy work, maybe tell them this story. The good people always survive. The despots do not.

In Good People: The Only Leadership Decision That Really Matters, Author Anthony Tjan talks about the Good People Mantra.[ix] No fancy acronyms, but it's very powerful.

BE people first

HELP others become the fullest version of themselves

COMMIT beyond competency to the values of goodness

BALANCE the realities and tensions of goodness

PRACTICE goodness whenever possible, not just when tested

Being a good leader tomorrow starts with being good to people today.

49. I'm Too Busy to Lead

I'm not going to lie. I often tune out when other leaders say they are too busy. No matter what comes after, I tend to stop listening at that point.

When someone on my team says it, it's one thing. I can work with them to re-prioritize and rearrange their workload, so they are not overwhelmed.

But when someone entrusted with a team and budgets says they are too busy on numerous occasions, perhaps that leader needs some coaching, or should not be at the helm of a department or team.

But it's not even the "too busy" part that gets me upset; it's the "too busy to lead" part that irks me. That means they have too many emails and not enough time for their people. It means they are in too many damned meetings and are not making enough time for their people. It could also mean they suck at time management.

At almost every company I have worked at, I have witnessed this happen. Leaders:

- Are too busy to meet with and correct the underperformer in their area

- Are too busy to do a yearly performance evaluation

- Do not have enough time for daily or weekly team huddles

- Do not have enough time in their day— again, a time block would help—for a one-on-one coffee with a team member to see if their development is on the right course

I've tried helping some of my contemporaries when I hear these things, telling them it's all about priorities, and giving them some helpful hints, or even a book or two to read. It's helped a couple, but the majority think that's way harder than sticking with the status quo.

As a leader, if you are too busy to lead people, then just manage tasks and pass the honour of leading your people onto someone else—someone who will figure it out and *make* time for their team.

50. You Can't Fight Pride

If your boss—or a higher-level executive like the CEO, or even one of your contemporaries—has an idea or plan and it is based on pride, you have a very slim chance of changing their mind. Even with data. Even with the best intentions. Even with daily coffees and gifts. Pride is a tough fight.

I once wanted to make a decision on a technology vendor I thought would be the perfect fit for our company and where we were on our growth journey.

However, IT didn't report to me. And while I knew (and everyone knew) this technology could be a game-changer for our company, the executive IT reported into wanted it to be their decision and they wanted to lead the process from beginning to end.

But it wasn't a skill-set or knowledge-based reason. It was about pride in owning that mandate. And as soon as I understood that, there was no business case or PowerPoint in the world that was going to change their mind (believe me, I tried about five times in different ways).

The point is, once you realize pride is in the way, handle with care or just let it go, and go on to the next project. It won't be worth the frustration to fight pride with fire (or data).

(And just to note, in this particular case, we ended up selecting the technology my team and I wanted all along. And our team also ended up leading that project. Some time was wasted in waiting to be sure, but it all ended up okay.)

51. Do You Have an Ownership Culture?

Many leaders say things like:

"Be accountable."

"This is your budget."

"This is your decision."

"Act as if this were your business."

Or something similar.

And then you know what they do? They micromanage the crap out of every decision their team makes or ask for numerous approvals on the way to the launch of a project or product, or even just the making of a decision. If you have a "drive the bus like it's yours" culture, you can't be an autocrat. Many organizations want to get to an "ownership" culture but are not willing to give up some authority and sense of control. You have to decide what you want for you and your team.

And it's okay if you don't want an ownership culture. But then you can't say "this is your decision" or "run it like it's your business or money." Your team is not perfect. And they will trip up from time to time. They will potentially fall and get some scrapes along the way. But if they are truly held accountable and made to feel like it was their decision in the first place, they will get back up in no time.

If you do live and breathe the ownership culture, as many successful companies and leaders do, you will have happier and more dedicated employees.

If you have happy and dedicated employees, you will generally have a thriving business.

You can't train passion. You can train for job skills, but I'll take passion and dedication as top attributes any day. To have accountable employees, you need to give accountability.

52. Sometimes You Have to Tell, Not Ask

As you gain more confidence in your career, have more comfort and trust in your boss, and truly understand the needs of your business, you'll start telling a story and saying what you will do, rather than asking for approval or budget to move the project forward.

There are little subtleties in language it helps to keep in mind. Some examples:

Not Good:
We have it in the budget to spend $150K on media in the Fall. Just making sure we can still spend it?

Way Better:
We are going to be spending $150k on media this Fall to generate $600k in incremental sales, or a 4x return on ad spend.

Not Good:
I was wondering if you agree to overhaul our technology. It will cost about $50k. I just can't get any more out of this technology anymore, and it's costing my team and me tons of time.

Way Better:
We have an efficiency problem. But I know how to solve it. There's an amazing technology that is

perfect for us, and they want to partner with us. In fact, it's only going to cost us $50k for the year. There will be cost savings in gaining efficiencies of about $200k, not to mention the increase in sales it will lead to. We plan on launching in three months.

Not Good:
I know when I started, we spoke about adding three headcounts, and while I may not need them this week, I really feel like we need a larger team to get to the next level. Can we hire the three people?

Way Better:
We're going to be a leader in this category. We've grown 5x from last year already, and this is with many inefficiencies. We also outsource way too much. I propose to bring this internal and hire three people. Firstly, we'll get more output. Secondly, we'll save $400k next year.

Make the case work for you. And don't make up any numbers or facts. They must be true. But tell a story and don't ask for permission. Tell your leadership team what you plan on doing.

53. Can You Call That Communication?

Just because you sent an email does not mean you communicated properly, or that your team truly understood your message.

George Bernard Shaw said it well:

"The single biggest problem in communication is the illusion that it has taken place."

As leaders, we often think that because we sent a text, an email, or an instant message, we can checkmark that the communication has occurred, or we can think we are great communicators.

Good communication is the clear understanding of the message, not the medium we use to send it. It's a good reflex to remind ourselves and inquire of the team "is the ask clear?" or "does everyone understand the project?"

Remember this as you climb the ranks: you need to be a great communicator to be a good leader.

54. Attitude is Everything

Hold yourself in the manner you want to be respected for. But remember you will never be criticized for having a positive attitude.

I've worked for many bosses, some of whom were positive, others who were at times killjoys or control freaks. I think you can guess which bosses I had more fun working for.

American businessman and philanthropist William Clement Stone was spot on the money when he said:

"Sales are contingent upon the attitude of the salesman, not the attitude of the prospect."

Whether it's selling a product, a service, or a vision, your team and customers are more apt to buy and believe—and want to work with—someone who has a great attitude over the curmudgeon. You can't be both. Choose wisely.

55. A Stern Fist is Not Always Needed

I once had an employee on my team who was an amazing worker but who was having a tough week.

Deadlines were missed. Excuses were made about not receiving emails and they were mixing updates and timelines.

When I forwarded this employee all the things they had missed, with dates and clear instructions, they felt horrible. This employee knew they had made a mistake. They knew they had messed up. I said we caught it early enough and let's learn from it and be better organized.

You know what the employee said? "Thank you for not scolding me. I messed up, and you helped me learn rather than making me feel even worse."

And make no mistake, I was disappointed in the work not being done, or my ask not being followed originally. But I was never going to yell and scream at this employee, who happened to be having a rough week.

And when this employee said that to me, and said their previous boss would not have let it go without numerous putdowns, it made me wonder:

How often do bosses scold, and not teach?

How often do managers raise their voices in an effort to be heard, but instead, have their words fall on deaf ears?

How many leaders overreact to mistakes, and rather than inspire their team, they take the wind out of their sails?

When your team members make a mistake, try to teach so they learn, rather than yell and demotivate them.

56. The Alignment Exercise

I once worked at a company where we had engaged the services of a consulting agency to try to help us build a three-year strategic plan and also align all departments towards a similar vision.

This agency had a great question: they asked our president "what does alignment look like, or mean, for you?"

The president had an equally great answer. He said: "if we got our leadership team together in a few months, and asked them 20 questions, and they all had very similar answers on our business goals and strategies, that would be alignment for me."

I think it's a great way to look at it, and one you can take to your teams. I think 20 questions may be too high, but if you stick around the 10-question mark, that should be something you and your team strive for – to all have similar answers to questions about values, what the company/departments stand for, processes, sales targets, and BHAGs (Big, Hairy, Audacious, Goals) in the next three years.

Often people talk about alignment but don't truly define it. This Alignment Exercise is a great way to do so.

57. Positive Words Can Mean the World

Do you remember when you were first starting out in your career, and you had to present in a meeting that was to include senior executives, including your boss? And then you found out the owner or CEO would be present as well? Gulp.

Fast forward through all the anxiety, and you absolutely rocked the presentation; everyone left the room impressed, and they all knew your name. But your boss never said anything to you. Nothing positive. Nothing negative.

Well, let me tell you: when one of your employees—or any young professional starting out at your company—finds themselves in the same situation, make sure you tell them how great it went, and what a great job they did. It will make their day and they'll remember it for years. And it will give them so much confidence.

Also be proud you had a hand in helping them rock that presentation. In these cases, mum's not the word; give them the encouragement they so badly desire.

58. Common Traits of Successful Leaders

I like to understand what makes successful people tick.

What motivates them?

How did they become successful?

What are their challenges?

What are their accomplishments?

How do they celebrate their wins?

What feeds their hunger?

How do they balance family and work?

And so on.

In my reading about—and my non-scientific studies of—successful people, I am constantly brought back to three traits, or habits if you will, that they all share.

In no particular order:

1. Successful people wake up early.

2. Successful people read (a lot).

3. Successful people meditate.

Let's unpack these.

The Early Bird Gets the Worm
Successful people don't have more time than anyone else. But they gain an hour or two by waking up super early (between 5:00 a.m. and 6:30 a.m.), whereas many people wake up after 6:30 a.m.

And successful and driven people prioritize their day in order of most to least important tasks and/or meetings. So, it often feels like successful people have more time, but they have just become experts in time management. (As a side note, many successful people wake up early to start their day with a workout, which also shows their drive and dedication to maintaining a healthy lifestyle and taking on challenges.)

Successful people do *work*, not *hours*. People often fail because they do *too many* things, inefficiently. The most successful people do great things efficiently, thus they seem to be more productive—and push forward more—than those who don't manage work effectively.

Said another way, they get the most out of the time they have in a day.

Reading Equals Learning

Have you ever read autobiographies or articles about the richest people, the top CEOs, or the best leaders in combat? Successful leaders read. A ton. Books, articles, blogs, periodicals—they crave information and knowledge, and they also do a great job of using what they learn.

Sometimes they read for entertainment, but more often than not, they are in hot pursuit of knowledge in order to improve something about themselves or their company.

If you don't read, or don't read often enough, make it your habit this year. Start with the goal of reading two books per month, in essence, 24 books per year. If that is too hard, then start with reading one book per month, or 12 books per year, which anyone could and should be doing. Once this becomes easy, you'll be thankful this is one of your habits.

Meditation is a Practice. Practice it Daily

We sleep to rest our bodies. We medicate to cure a cold or headache. We exercise to get fit. But how do we rest our minds? How do we make it a practice to stay in the present moment more often? Successful people know that a clear and non-stressed mind is a great advantage and a powerful accelerator in their pursuit of great achievement.

Meditation is often their answer. Whether it's three, five, or 30 minutes per day, meditation is a form of clearing your mind by focusing on your breath, an object, or an activity. Meditation helps to train focus and awareness while being emotionally calm and mentally clear. Whatever you end up using it for, the practice of meditation really has no negatives.

Find the time to meditate, and your mind will be better rested, sharper, and less foggy—which all result in better decision-making, whether it's in your personal or professional life.

Again, these three common traits are witnessed over and over. And this does not mean that if you don't do these you can't be successful. I know a few very successful people who wake up later in the morning and are night owls, for example. What I'm saying is that these three traits, when combined, may make the success journey a bit easier.

59. Do You Let Others Make Mistakes?

This one is not for the weak of heart— or the perfectionist—but there are times when I let members of my team fail.

Yes, there have been situations where I know what they are proposing will not work. And if the mistake, error, or outcome is not too serious, I sometimes let that individual make it.

Granted, sometimes the employee in question is not the best listener and they have tons of pride, and they have a "please trust me" attitude. "Okay, then," I think, "Go do it your way."

Inevitably, two weeks later, they are back at my desk and we're trying to figure out what went wrong. If this happens early, as in the first year of employment, this is a real positive. Do you think that employee will ever make that mistake again? Their pride may have taken a hit, but that's when your supreme leadership skills step in to build them back up again.

I love confident people, but sometimes, one of your team members is overly confident and won't listen to you or reason with you. They believe in their way. So let them fall (be strategic on when that first fall is) and then, be there after they fall and come around to chat.

It's not the time for *I-told-you so's*—they've come to seek help. Support them, don't berate them.

Never say, "I told you so." Turn these experiences into great positive and learning situations. The employee who just made that mistake? He or she will be your next superstar.

60. Always Think Beyond Yourself

A former employee of mine was once out of a job. He's a very driven person and an incredibly talented guy. But there was a downturn in his industry, and he was let go.

I let many of my contemporaries know through private messages that if they were hiring, he'd be a great candidate for any of their roles.

Lo and behold, two days later my former employee had several interviews lined up. He sent me a thank you note.

This is something I've done often for people in my network and will continue to do. And I always get a thank you. It's rewarding for me, and words can't even express the feeling I get from giving someone a hand when they need it.

Pay it forward, always. Be kind to others and help them out when they need you the most.

61. Attention: Get It, Keep It

As a leader you tell stories. Not the make-believe kind; but you tell stories so people believe in you, so you motivate and inspire them, so you tell them what may or may not work.

Peter Gruber, a media and movie executive and author, told an interesting story in his book, *Tell to Win: Connect, Persuade, and Triumph with the Hidden Power of Story*. He was on a rafting trip and his group was not paying much attention to the life and death stakes facing them if something went wrong.

Richard Bangs was a guest on their expedition, but also owned a company called Sobel Expeditions. The group was not taking much seriously, so Richard told them this tale:

> *"Three thousand years ago, the first King of Egypt – a notorious asshole, was screwing around during a hunting party and so pissed off his dogs that they turned on him. The pack chased him all the way to the Nile [R]iver, which was infested with crocodiles.*
> *One of these huge reptiles lay sunning itself on the bank. It offered to ferry the King across the river, and he was so desperate he agreed.*
> *To his surprise, the croc actually did take him safely across, but then his saviour revealed that*

he was Sobek, the crocodile spirit. In return for saving the King's life, Sobek demanded some serious change.

The King had to wisen up and lead his people to treat the river and all its creatures with due respect. As long as the humans paid homage, their boats would be granted safe passage.[x]

Whoa. Ya, if I was on that expedition, I would stop talking the rest of the trip and just be cautious of my surroundings. It's a great story (and *Tell to Win* is a great book on how to connect, persuade, and triumph with words) and that's the reason Bangs named his company Sobek Expeditions, after the crocodile spirit.

Sometimes, you need to use great storytelling, or shock value, to get your point across. This is especially true when you know you can't fail on a project, but your team does not appear focused; or when no other conversation has worked with an employee whose next slip is a pink one; or when your team needs a good wake up call.

Great (leadership) storytelling is an art. Study it and practice it. It will serve you well.

62. Encourage, Don't Discourage

I enjoy public speaking. That wasn't always the case. But once I challenged myself into it, it really became something I loved.

For those who have spoken in front of an audience, big or small, there is a nervousness, or "butterflies in the stomach" type of feeling, akin to playing sports, right before a big game. All of this is to say, I've never seen public speaking *not* make someone into a better professional. You would think most companies would embrace that.

Well, I once worked at a very large enterprise, and when I was hired, I was very upfront, and said I often speak and do podcasts, and I have my own blog. They were okay with that. I was a senior leader, but still a couple of positions removed from the C-Suite.

After one or two speaking engagements in my second year of employment, I began to hear rumblings that the C-suite didn't love the fact that I spoke, as they felt they should be the mouthpiece, the only ones allowed to speak. I actually wasn't even speaking about the company, but more on the topics of digital marketing, retail, and Ecommerce, or more generally, digital transformation.

Think about how that made me feel. Here I was, working my butt off for them, and also practicing my public speaking, getting "free" publicity for this company (as I always spoke highly of them when chatting in between sessions with others while at these types of events), yet I felt some sort of hierarchical push-back (maybe jealousy?) about the fact I was getting speaking engagements.

On more than one occasion, I would get a negative nudge about taking on another speaking engagement, something like "hey, are you sure you want to speak at that event? Our CEO and CMO think you're getting too much airtime."

Too much airtime? My career was on the upswing, and here I was being discouraged from doing something I loved. This was a bit hypocritical considering how much this company supported education and advancement, at least publicly. And I always got my presentations approved by my bosses, as well as the PR and HR departments. They always loved them.

The message here is to encourage your employees to pursue extracurricular activities, not to discourage them. Now, they should never be sharing confidential or sensitive information. But beyond that, you should be encouraging your employees to pursue speaking, philanthropy, playing guitar in a band, whatever it may be. You should be there to motivate them, and not discourage them.

63. Don't Make the Interview Stuffy

Too often, we get a managerial role and then we feel like we yield the ultimate power – hiring and firing. While that may be somewhat true, don't make your interviews stuffy.

When you interview a candidate, you want them to be as comfortable as possible. You want them to be open and honest and show their great side.

You want the right fit. But if they are tense and playing defence the entire time, how will you ever get to know them? How would you treat a first date? It's a similar process when interviewing. Make them feel welcome.

A former employee of mine, a superstar who is going to do great things, sent me a note recently. In it, he said he'd gone through numerous interviews since we'd initially had ours.

He said no one else has come close to making him feel how I did in that interview. He also said many hiring managers he's interviewed with seem doubtful of his accomplishments, and the hiring managers were more negative than positive.

1. I was really touched by his note. But …

2. Managers, and leaders in general, need to be better. If we're making budding superstars feel like they should be honoured just to even get the chance to interview with us/them, maybe it's time to look in the mirror.

Make your interviewee feel at ease, compliment them, show your passion, be positive, don't cut them off when they speak, don't embarrass them, and truly listen.

You may be higher ranking, but that gives you no right to demean them. Afterall, you were in their position not too long ago.

64. Help a Struggling Colleague in Need

You have every right to look after your team. But as a growing leader, you also have a right to help colleagues who are not on your team. That may sound obvious, but many leaders choose to close their eyes.

If you have solid people skills, you'll know some of the employees who may be struggling, either with the workload or, more often, with their boss.

Some of these employees may not even like coming to work anymore. They are staying because they have few options, but they are becoming desolate.

Take them aside. Get to know them. Ask how you can help. Often times, they may not have the courage to talk directly to their manager. But maybe you could help. Maybe you could talk to their manager. Heck, maybe you can transfer this employee to your team.

I've mentored a few employees like this. And within a couple of months, most of them passionately joined my team or department, or got the courage to speak to their boss. Why? Because I genuinely helped them and figured out what they were passionate about, and maybe even what their boss wasn't doing well with them.

Sometimes it was as simple as leaving a book on their desk, or suggesting a podcast they should listen to, or guiding them towards a free event Google was hosting.

Another time, I asked if this employee was willing to learn another completely different role in order to get out from under the manager they hated so much.

I sent them a course to take. Within weeks, they were signed up. This showed me the dedication and hunger this employee still had. They just needed someone to believe in, and who in turn believed in them, and someone who inspired them.

You're reading this. Be. That. Person. We need more of them.

65. Learning, Always

Ray Dalio wrote this in his fine book, *Principles: Life and Work*:

"It seems to me that if you look back on yourself a year ago and aren't shocked at how stupid you were, you haven't learned much."[xi]

Now, this does not mean you may be further from your goal today than you were one year ago. It's not to say today is better than 365 days ago, because you could slip backwards at times. We all do. But I'm sure you learned a thing or two about yourself in that year.

If you have stopped learning and growing, you need to get out of the rut, and get back on track. Most successful leaders—and almost all successful people—realize they have learned so much in a year.

Now, the key to this is tracking. Write your goals down and review them, do some daily, weekly, or monthly journaling, or ensure you self-reflect every few months at the very least. If you want to get ahead, you need to know where you were, and what's up ahead, and do all you can in the present to ensure you take the past and leverage it to make a better future.

Learning is key on your journey. Start today. Challenge yourself to be better in the next 90 days. Do something tangible that ensures that when you look back, you'll know if you're ahead of where you were 90 days ago.

The turning point for me was when I started setting yearly goals, which I broke into monthly, weekly, and daily tasks.

I knew which milestones I needed to hit. I then layered in self-reflection, positive affirmations, and journaling, with weekly reviews of my short-term and long-term goals, and what I had accomplished in the previous seven days to get there.

Another added benefit of tracking is how proud you can feel when you look back and see how much you accomplished and grew in such a short period of time. It's a life-changer.

66. Workload no excuse for bad treatment

From time to time, everyone has a bad day. From the CEO to the human resources (HR) manager to Positive Suzie in Accounting. But I never want to hear you blame what you did, what you said, or how you said it, on stress caused by your workload.

Check yourself. If you are overwhelmed, hey, that happens. But close your office door, take the day off to catch up, go for a drive, try meditating, or whatever else you need to do. Never treat people badly because you have too much work. If that's the case, start your own company, don't hire anyone, and do all the work yourself.

Everyone has bad days. But don't take it out on your staff. And if you do, you *need* to apologize within 24 hours, or you may lose respect forever.

Think about the trickle effect your shitty day and poor attitude have had on your employees: you ruined their day, they then went home sullen, which likely ruined their spouse's night, and then their kids saw how upset they were, and *they* got sad. This employee then messaged one or two employees and told them how they were treated, and now it's building steam and spiralling.

If you are overwhelmed because of your workload or meetings or lack of time, don't take it out on your team. That's not leadership. That's being a jerk.

67. The 70/20/10 Rule of Development

Most companies follow and adhere to a 70/20/10 rule when it comes to employee development. This is a super straight forward development mechanism. But inaction is the enemy. You can alter any part of this program to make it your own but make sure to action this for your employees (and yourself!).

70% of your time should be spent on working in and developing your current role, including your assigned projects and tasks. This is about getting better and better at your day-to-day tasks. Essentially, this is what you were hired to do.

20% of your time should be spent learning within the company, be it spending time with senior leaders or subject matter experts, working with coaches, or speaking frequently with external agencies or organizations. Think of this as education during your 9-5 workday.

10% of your time should be spent educating yourself: training to acquire new skills, getting new certifications or diplomas, and/or gaining knowledge to advance to the next level. This is generally planning and education on your own time. While much of this can be expensed back to the company, these activities often happen *after* work hours. The onus is on you. (If you're lucky, you can manage to squeeze some in during your workday, too).

68. Selecting Your Team

Do you remember in gym class when you were the captain, and you had to choose a team, one by one, and you hoped the other captain wouldn't choose the best athletes, or your best friends? You wanted them all to yourself. Well, when you lead a team in the business world, it's not so different.

With a large caveat: make sure your team lives by the same values you do.

Whether it's your best friend, the smartest guy you know, or the best engineer you've ever seen, if they don't espouse similar core values to those that you have, it won't be much of a team.

That's not to say you don't need diversity; you absolutely do need different perspectives and personality traits on a team. But think of this as just one example of value: when challenges arise and problems persist, how are they dealt with? Truthfully? Buried? Hidden? And if critical feedback is given, do they carry a grudge?

Famed Dutch economist Dr. Albert Winsemius is said to have attributed part of his success in building great teams to creating a diversity of excellence but commonality in character and values to ensure high-performing teams.

I would 100% agree with that.

Trust. Character. Values. Spirit. You can teach all other elements, but these qualities are generally inherent in a person.

Choose wisely. If some of these traits are your core values, you likely don't want employees who live by polar opposite values.

69. Good to Great

The really good leaders work on their leadership, their communication, and on their personal development, constantly. But the great leaders spend as much time developing and helping their team, as they do on themselves.

Author Anthony Tjan said it perfectly in his book, *Good People*:

"...It all begins at the top, with leaders who are unafraid to show compassion in their leadership approach. These leaders understand that only by working as hard to realize others' potential as they work to realize their own can they transform entire industries, cultivate vibrant cultures, and produce enduring value."[xii]

Work on yourself, constantly. Always try to develop yourself personally.

But the great leaders not only work on themselves, they also help their teams daily – to help their employees be better than they were the day before.

A true leader is selfless and cares about the greater good.

So, today, send each of your team members a note and ask them to outline their current goals or maybe a current issue you can help them solve. Make them better.

70. Stand Behind Your Team

I once worked at a company that was using one of the largest media agencies in the world. We paid them quite well, but I personally didn't find we were getting their A-team.

In fact, an issue around their professionalism came to a head one day. One of their employees had mistakenly included one of my team members in an email that was meant to be internal. In it, the agency employee made a disparaging comment about the intelligence and digital knowledge of this team member.

That was the last day that person was on our account. When my team told me about the email, I read it and was absolutely irate. I went to all three levels above this agency employee and had an immediate call. Level-headed, I said this employee will never work on one of our accounts again. This employee's bosses were embarrassed and apologetic. And my team really appreciated that I had no tolerance for any type of disrespect toward them.

You gain or lose respect in these types of circumstances. Always stand up for your team when others do wrong.

71. An Idea for Personal / Vacation Days

At some point in your career, you will have some team members who don't need or want to take vacation days or any personal days. Often, they are single, they enjoy coming to work, and they don't feel they need a break.

So, when vacation days start to accumulate, I send them to a local event or, better yet, an out-of-town conference, and ask them to tack on a couple of days for sightseeing.

Be a transformative leader and think about how you can help your team be better. Rest makes your employees better. Just like an athlete needs rest to recuperate, an employee needs rest to refresh and reenergize. And they'll be thankful for it.

72. Think of How a Doctor Would Act

Doctors usually don't beat around the bush when dealing with a patient's illness. And they shouldn't. They need to be honest and transparent. But the excellent doctors understand compassion. It's no different in leadership.

If all you're trying to do is get ahead, and burn some bridges along the way, with little empathy for the employees you leave behind, karma may eventually find you.

But if you lead with compassion and empathy, you will lead a team that *wants* to follow you and that *wants* to make you succeed. Teams that *want* to follow their leader require less time to buy into the project, mission, vision, or goals of the department/company.

So, when the next challenge arises, be like a good doctor, and show empathy and compassion while being honest.

73. Some 5,000+ Failures to Perfection

James Dyson is known for helping to create one of the best vacuums in history, the Dyson. A little-known fact is that it took 5,127 prototypes before he got it right. So that's 5,126 times he failed. I'd say, that's 5,126 times he learned how to do it better. Dyson also uttered one of the best quotes I've ever heard on the topic of failure:

"I've always thought that school children should be marked by the number of failures they've had. The child who tries strange things and experiences lots of failures to get there is probably more creative…We're taught to do things the right way. But if you want to discover something that other people haven't, you need to do things the wrong way."[xiii]

This may ring true for you. It may hit a nerve. You also may have an employee who is always trying things in a different way yet fails more than others. Maybe this helps you be more patient with them or support them even further. After all, they could be the next James Dyson or Elon Musk. Just think, "they are X number of tries away from a masterpiece."

74. Addition By Subtraction

Remove people who put you down. Those who drag you down and don't propel you have no place in your successful life.

This may be one of the most important passages of this book. If this person happens to be a close family member or boss, try removing them from your life as much as possible for one week.

Stay away from them as much as you can; maybe go on vacation without any contact with them.

I know it's easier said than done, but if you find certain people in your network or family are pulling you down, are jealous of you, or block your energy with negativity, remove them from your life, temporarily—until they change—or permanently, if they don't change.

You need to be around positive people who propel and motivate you, not the opposite. Start by making a list of who you need to be spending less time with, and who you should probably be spending more time with. And then start slowly actioning against that list. Take it week by week.

75. Above and Beyond, and Then Some

There may be days when you ask yourself, "when will all this work pay off?"

"When will my extra-long weeknights get me something?"

"When will catching up on emails during the weekend impress my boss?"

"When will the 50+ hours of work I put in get me that promotion?"

There is a quote I love that many people have attributed to motivational speaker Zig Ziglar. It makes this idea seem even more mysterious, yet powerful.

"If you are willing to do more than you are paid to do, you will eventually be paid more for what you do."

Trust the process. It will pay off.

If you are positive, kind, have great values and character, are passionate about what you do, and have a strong work ethic, you will climb the ranks, you will be successful, and at some point along the way, you will be paid very well to do it, either by your boss, your investors, or your customers.

Everyone's career is different, but there will be a Tipping Point, where you know the hard work *has* paid off. Trust the process.

76. Advice on Talking Too Much

Here's the truth. I am skeptical when people talk a lot during interviews, like they are trying to sell something.

It may be nerves (which I can deal with), but if you keep talking about a question and simply go in circles and not really answer it, be careful, as your subject may have faded out of the conversation.

Now, as the person being interviewed, you absolutely must tell your story, but make it memorable rather than wordy. Don't ramble. Also, the interviewee needs to understand if the company is right for them, so make sure you ask questions and listen to the answers intently.

In meetings, I am also skeptical when the same few people have *too much* to say. You likely can name a few in your organization.

Unless you are leading the meeting, if you are a participant and try to steal the show with words rather than impact, you are hurting yourself way more than helping.

Leaders get skeptical of other leaders who talk too much, those people who use way too many words but don't really say anything of substance.

It's almost as if they are trying to prove their worth, their role, or their knowledge.

There are certain times when you need to dive in and perhaps even provide verbose explanations, but know your audience, know the point of the meeting, and don't waste other people's time trying to prove your worth. It does the opposite.

77. Inheriting a Team Like Buying House

Have you ever bought a house you didn't build yourself? Or moved into a place that has already been lived in?

If you have, you know the feeling of seeing all the imperfections that exist and wanting to do everything on Day One.

But you don't. You let the leaky faucet leak for a few days before calling the plumber. You unpack all your boxes and then re-arrange the furniture a number of times before getting it just right. You paint before hanging all your picture frames and wall art. Said another way, it's very hard to do everything on Day One, especially if you are moving in with your family.

It's not that different from starting your leadership role at another company and inheriting a team that's been there for some time. You can't expect them to change or adhere to your style on Day One, or even Week One.

It will also take some time for you to get to know your employees, really know them, once you finally build some trust with them.

So, you should let time settle things down before making any rash decisions on people in general, or those on your team. Have a couple of meetings with each team member, test them out, see if they are open to change and mentorship.

Then, if after a few weeks or months you still feel like they are not a good fit on your team and for the future of the business, let them go.

But you owe it to them and your company to allow things to settle before making quick decisions on human capital.

78. Ranking Your Values is Critical

Many companies have values. They have a mission statement. A vision. A purpose. They understand their Why, What, and How.

Some make them simple, and some make them fancy and complex—to the point where no one remembers what they are.

But once you set your vision (for a company, or your team, or even for your own life, for that matter), it's crucial you have values and principles that guide your behaviour while you attempt to succeed in business, as a leader, or in life.

But if values are not ordered and ranked, there may be unforeseen issues that will arise.

Here are a couple of examples.

Say you rank the profitability of the company as your #1 Value, and your second most important value is being kind. Since #1 (Profitability) comes before being kind to your team, colleagues, or vendors, what can happen is a winner-take-all-effect, where employees just concentrate on quarterly profits and leave feelings and culture in the dust.

Another example may be a company whose values are centred on kindness, culture, doing right, saying no to the status quo, and finding solutions. But nowhere does it list profits, sales, winning, being among the top three in market share in your industry, or anything based on performance. And that is also not being realistic—unless maybe you're a non-profit organization—nor true to what the shareholders, owners, or the CEO want.

So, it's important your values include what you want to stand for, how you carry yourself, and that you understand how that fits into fulfilling your vision on a day-to-day basis.

However, without ordering and ranking your values by priority, they can become just words on a page that may lead to confusion and a lack of alignment.

79. Pay a Premium for Great Talent

If you were moving, and had some expensive furniture and electronics that needed to be moved to your new house, would you seek the lowest-priced company to help you move?

Or, if you're going on a date or taking your spouse out for a 10th-anniversary celebration, would you select the cheapest bottle of wine on the menu?

I really and truly hope you answered, "of course not, Johnny!" – especially with regards to the wine example! But in all seriousness, when did securing or recruiting talent become about getting the cheapest person out there?

I've been recruited or involved in recruiting, and I know HR teams need to stay within a budget. They are often unwilling to budge by a mere $5k or $10k, even if that meant securing a talented individual who would provide savings or sales of more than 10x that amount in their first six months.

I'm all for budgeting, and I recognize each company needs to follow a certain hierarchy for salaries. But why do companies so often settle on talent because candidates #1 and #2 were $10k over budget? So, you settle for #3, because he asked to be remunerated less than your top threshold? Maybe there was a reason for that—namely, that the other two candidates are that much better! Additionally, they likely have a higher market value.

If you're expecting three or four years of tenure when you hire a candidate, pay the premium upfront when it makes sense.

The odds are likely in your favour this candidate will work out a bit (or a lot) better than the #3 choice you hired to fit into your budget. If it upsets the salary hierarchy in your organization, maybe the hierarchy needs to be revisited, or, maybe you need to find a more creative way to structure the contract with bonuses, expense accounts, or other monetary stick-handling.

Take the small risk and pony up for talent that stands out from the field. It's a competitive advantage. Do you know why? People are your most critical competitive advantage. Treat them as such.

80. Too Busy - Except for Complaining

I bet many of you are already nodding your head. You likely know many of these employees—the ones who bitch and complain about everything and anything, who are the captains of the negativity committee. I sincerely hope you are not one of those people.

And if you are one of those negative people, *and* you're in a leadership position, you need to listen up. If you are always "too busy," every week in a 52-week year, doesn't it occur to you to think something is wrong? Maybe your boss is giving you work you cannot handle, maybe your company is driving you mad or, maybe, the problem is you.

I've been at companies where senior leaders have said they were too busy, and HR tried helping by telling them they would hire people to ease the workload. The leader's response? "That won't help either, as we're too busy to train them."

That mentality has "lose" written all over it, as you are going to lose in work and in life.

You cannot be overwhelmed every single day and manage a successful team. If you have too many tasks, that is likely your own fault.

By saying yes to everything that comes your way—and believing you can do it all—you're hurting your own career and your team's belief in you if you don't carry these out successfully.

Either say no to some tasks or, even better, prioritize your tasks in order of importance, or in order of the importance of the person (in terms of rank) asking for them. CEOs generally outrank everyone, right?

And the cherry on top is that sometimes the people who complain about having no time will spend 30 minutes each day complaining to their nearest colleague about their workload and their evil boss. If you have extra time to complain about being too busy, why don't you try using that time to do some work?

Prioritize your tasks, weeks, and days, and you'll be complaining less about being too busy; you'll also be spending more time working your way to a promotion. If you believe you are on the negativity committee, try your best to relinquish that role to others.

81. Accentuate the Positive

Sometimes as leaders we think we need to catch our team doing something wrong or incorrect in order to steer them in the right direction. And to some degree, being a leader is about correcting wrongs because you may have more experience than your employees. But a true leader focuses on the positive more often than not.

In their book, *Helping People Win at Work: A Business Philosophy Called "Don't Mark My Paper, Help Me Get an A,"* Ken Blanchard and Garry Ridge call Accentuating the Positive the ultimate coaching tool. Blanchard is spot on when he writes:

> "If someone told me, 'Going forward, you can't teach anything you have been teaching over the past 40 years except one thing,' what I would hold onto is this: The key to developing people is to catch them doing something right."[xiv]

It's one of those leadership traits that sounds obvious but is rarely practiced. We take it for granted. We've all been there when someone we respect tells us what a great job we did, or that we're on the right track with our project. We feel so good and positive in that moment, and it builds on the confidence we may have had.

"It is important to remember," Blanchard continues on the topic, "that you should not wait until people do something perfectly right to praise them. Praise progress, because it's a moving target."[xv]

Do it today. Catch your team doing something right. Show your team that small and large moments of positive encouragement and kindness can win in business. It's not soft. It's human-centred winning at its finest.

82. Create Your Matrix

Get out your tablet, mobile phone, or pen and paper. Let's create your matrix. No, not the movie, and not your organization's matrix. Your own matrix of life. It's based on the Wheel of Change created by Marshall Goldsmith.[xvi]

I've read a number of books that cross over into these four main sections (Create, Preserve, Eliminate, and Accept) that I am asking you to work on, and I find this is the best and easiest way to get the information out of you.

See the chart below (or create something similar). Be sure to change the year for the current one.

Then, in the spaces provided below, fill in your Creating, Preserving, Eliminating, and Accepting habits, for both Personal and Work life.

For more clarity on what they each mean:

- **Creating** (i.e., adding/inventing) for work could be to create the best department culture in the company. And having each member of the team learn to be a future leader

- **Preserving** (i.e., keeping/maintaining) for personal could be to preserve the ambition, optimism, and perseverance you have

- **Eliminating** (i.e., eradicating/reducing) for work could be to eliminate the meetings you have by 20%

- **Accepting** (i.e., delaying/making peace) for personal could be to accept that the weather won't be perfect every day

My only advice is to try and keep it to one-to-three habits for each. This matrix could be for one year, two years, or even longer if you wish. I suggest reviewing this every year and seeing if you are on the right track, in both your personal and your work life, and see if anything needs to be edited or adjusted.

Your personal habits could include anything. From eating better, exercising more, reading more, walking the dog more often, not biting your nails, etc.

For the work matrix part, you might aim to create a better culture, attend fewer meetings, be better at prioritizing, ensure you always have an agenda for meetings, or accept that your unread inbox may never be at 0.

There is no right or wrong way to do this exercise, as long as you honestly and impactfully fill in the boxes.

Start writing. Make the first iteration a draft, and then fine-tune it and finalize it. It should take between 30 minutes and four hours to complete, depending on how self-aware you already are.

2022 Matrix		
	Personal	Work
Creating		
Preserving		
Eliminating		
Accepting		

83. Improve Performance Reviews System

I've worked for companies that had a performance scale for evaluating talent and giving, or not giving, raises.

I'm sure you're also familiar with it, as most companies continue to use this system. You know the one, where you must rate employees as excellent, average, or poor performers (or 10, 5, 1).

But here's the kicker. HR says you need some of your team members in each bucket. Even if they are all good.

If you rate them all as 9s and 10s, you'd be considered too soft a grader or manager.

If you give everyone on a failing team ratings of 1s and 2s, you'd basically be saying you can't motivate this bunch, so it's a poor reflection on you.

So, we blindly follow what was done before, because the system had to work. It got us here. That may be so, but there's a better way.

In the book *Whale Done: The Power of Positive Relationships*, Ken Blanchard, Thad Lacinak,

Chuck Tompkins, and Jim Ballard outline this exact problem with this beauty of a statement:

"If you don't hire people on a performance review curve, why grade them on one?"[xvii]

Which scenario below is likely to happen? And which one is better?

Scenario 1:
You know your boss can only rate one of his employees a 10 because of the historical departmental curve. He has five direct reports, and you are one of them. You each have goals to attain, and if you attain them, you'll increase your chances of getting that 10. But you will do so at all costs, including putting individual goals ahead of the team.

So, when it comes to helping a colleague and not getting any credit for it, you may just keep to yourself. Imagine an athlete who is more focused on individual awards and success than team ones. That is essentially how most companies set up their performance review systems.

Scenario 2:
The company states that team departmental goals are more important than individual ones, and to that end, there will be no curve. If you meet all your individual goals and your rather aggressive departmental goals, then you can all share in the

wealth, in terms of bonuses, to be sure, but you can also support each other in order to get stellar evaluation grades.

Since the departmental objectives must also be reached, that may cause most or all of your team members to be in the upper tier in terms of the rating system. And yes, that may mean they are all up for bonuses, but if they hit all their targets, why is that a bad thing?

I'd take Scenario 2, always. Why penalize people for doing great work, but because of a curve, they need to be rated downwards? How motivating is that?

And I think companies lose sight of that fact. They think because you get a "9," it means you're the next CEO. No, it means you had a really good quarter or a really good year, you accomplished all individual and team goals, and you were a great and positive influence on the company. What most companies forget is that you can rank high for a year of work, yet still have things to work on.

Today might be the day you work with your HR teams to discuss the performance rating system at your company.

If you're in HR, great! Help fix this system.

84. Company's Heartbeat: a Clear Vision

Do you ever show up for work feeling mostly anxious about the day or week ahead? That's kind of normal if it happens sometimes. However, does that feeling last every day, all month, and for the entire year? If so, then that's a huge red flag.

It might indicate that what you do for the company lacks meaning. Maybe your job satisfaction is low, or you're just not "feeling it."

In an endorsement for the book, *Full Steam Ahead* by Ken Blanchard and Jesse Stoner, business leader and franchise pioneer James H. Amos Jr. said:

> *"A clear vision gives an organization heart. Without it, work will have no meaning."[xviii]*

I think we've all been with a company whose vision was not clearly understood. But as a current and/or future leader, it's now your job to help shape and improve that vision.

Ensure there is clarity and alignment in the company's vision. Without a clear, focused, impactful vision for the company, it's likely you'll see a lot of sad faces walking in the hallways or on virtual calls.

85. The Secret to Creating More Time

Listen closely. Read this carefully. And memorize it…

There is no secret to creating more time. There are 24 hours in a day. That's all we have. Take out five-to-seven hours for sleeping, and we have even less. No, the secret is not in creating more time, it's in eliminating distractions.

You need to create more space in your life. That space will allow you to do more of what you love to do, more of what you want to do, more of what you need to do (like being a good family man/woman).

Maybe you talk endlessly on the phone, spend four hours a day on Facebook, Instagram, Tik-Tok, and other social media apps, maybe you watch Netflix for three hours every night, and six hours on weekends, maybe you watch the morning and nightly news (another two hours per day). Whatever form your distractions take, find a way to notice them, and then try eliminating them, by 20%, 50%, and if you want, more.

If you have a goal or goals which you are falling short in achieving—for example, reading two books per month, taking an online course, starting your own business, being a better dad or mom, being a better friend—find the things which are interfering with this, and remove them, either slowly, or suddenly, like a bandage.

I know for me, I used to eat, breathe, play, and watch sports.

As time got tighter, and family and work got more important, I played less sports (although I increased my fitness level with more gym time), read less on sports websites, and watched way less live sports than I had done previously. I also read less news (which I found ultra-negative) and spent less time talking on the phone (preferring text as a time-saver instead).

Even working mostly from home during the COVID-19 pandemic shaved off about 60-90 minutes of driving in traffic, which I could put into work or other things I needed to do. This all helped me gain so much more time to put into the projects I wanted to take on (like writing this book), or the person I wanted to become.

I exchanged time for time but became happier and more fulfilled. And I'm not saying you can't ever relax. And I'm not saying that chasing your purpose is easy. But if you choose your time and activities wisely, time will work for you, not against you.

You don't *find* extra time; you eliminate things that *take* your time.

86. Bet on Continuous Learning

A funny thing is happening in most industries: there is a drive to do more; there is a charge to fail fast; there is a desire for continuous learning.

But all that means more mistakes as we seek expertise in our employees and our leaders.

More risk equals potential for greater reward. But if that is the case, you must remember to be patient with people, because greater risk also means potentially greater failures and mistakes. Guide them. Help them swing for the fences.

Stealing from a baseball term, I've always said I would rather my team swing for the fences and try to hit homeruns—even if it means they strike out more often—than constantly hitting singles.

There's almost no such thing as an "expert" anymore. Things change so quickly that experts are really being seen as the people who are the best continuous learners. The fast pace of change basically ensures more people will be learning on the job. And that means more mistakes, which requires more patience.

The paradox lies in balancing the drive to change with performing at a high level so you can get results…while being patient. It takes a deft touch, but it can be done. And it *should* be done in order to drive long term results.

87. Show Kindness

Picture a CEO in your mind. Picture someone negotiating a contract. Picture a judge during a trial. Picture a cop giving out a ticket.

I bet you pictured someone stern. Someone harsh. Someone who might raise their voice. Someone who gets what they want. Someone who may even be somewhat impatient. Well, that may be the old school vision of a leader, but I can tell you that most great leaders of today and tomorrow are kind, compassionate, and listen more than they talk. My hope is the image of what it takes to be a successful leader of people changes from sternness to kindness.

A couple of years ago, my then-wife and I flew from Calgary to Toronto with our then-one-year-old son. After numerous flight delays, we arrived past midnight at Pearson Airport in Toronto. In epic timing, I had to be in Toronto for an interview with a large financial services corporation, and my wife had to attend the convocation for her master's degree in London, Ontario, about two hours away. We thought, "Perfect—we'll combine the commitments and make it all work in one trip."

We rented a car, and she took it upon herself to drive with our son to London, while I was to take the train to my downtown meet and greet. I was very early for my 8:00 a.m. meeting. I was reading quietly on the train at the terminal when my cell buzzed. It was my wife. The AVIS car rental manager was not allowing her to pick up the car I had booked for her under my name without physically seeing my ID. I had to bolt off the train before it left and head to the AVIS office in the airport a few minutes away. Once that was all settled and I helped my wife pack up the car, I found my way to the 7:30 a.m. train, which didn't leave until 7:40 a.m. I was cutting the meeting extremely close, so I messaged both HR and the hiring manager and explained my situation.

I arrived at their downtown headquarters about 10 minutes late for my meeting. I had one of the best interviews I've ever had with HR, and I had a great meeting with the hiring manager. But I still felt she was going to hold a grudge because I was late. That is usually inexcusable, but as far as reasons go, I had a good one. Did I mention that the meeting had originally been slated for 9:00 a.m., and the company had changed the time to 8:00 a.m. a couple of days earlier? Anyhow, I didn't get the job, and to this day, I am 99% sure it was because I was late for the interview.

Sure, it was a mistake to be late. But there are times when you need to be tough, and there are times to understand, be kind, be compassionate, and welcome talent that may be late for an interview, with good reason. I think they let a pretty good candidate walk away that day.

Now, many may disagree with me on this, but never let talent slip away because of old-school thinking.

88. Pace of Change – Fast and Slow

A favourite quote I share on a slide when I speak at events has been attributed to Canadian Prime Minister Justin Trudeau. In a speech at the World Economic Forum in Davos, Switzerland, in 2018, he said:

>*"The pace of change has never been this fast, and it will never be this slow again."*

Every time I read it, I love it even more. Take any moment in time, and this will have been true. Especially as we look at the super astronomical leaps of technology.

What we think is fast now, is just going to get quicker. And we will adapt. Let me correct that. The successful people will adapt.

Whether you're a parent, a couple with no kids, a professional, young, or old, your success will depend on how quickly you evolve and adapt to the changing pace of life.

So, embrace it. Take a deep breath, absorb it, adapt, and keep growing.

89. First Lead Yourself, then lead Many

If you are not self-aware, have difficulty making decisions, can't trust your team, or don't communicate well, you may need to look inward before becoming the leader you want to become.

It's rare for a leader to be so good they can lead an army yet have trouble leading and developing themselves.

In their book, *Helping People Win at Work*, Ken Blanchard and Garry Ridge talk about effective leadership being more than a destination. It's got many ups and downs, waves, and turns.

> *"I believe effective leadership is a journey,"* said Blanchard, *"beginning with self-leadership, moving to one-on-one leadership, and then team leadership, and then ending with organizational leadership."[xix]*

Indeed, it's a massive journey that is not perfect and tidy. Leadership can be messy.

But I concur with Blanchard when he says self-leadership is a must before you can become the quintessential leader you hope to one day be. I view it as lead One (yourself) before you can lead Two (yourself and one other team member), before you can lead many (a team) and, finally, before you can strategically and thoughtfully be a key leader to help drive your organization forward.

So, the sooner you can become the best version of yourself and understand your strengths, weaknesses, and what you need to work on, the sooner you can become an even more effective leader. And these don't all have to be linear. You can inherit a team before knowing yourself fully. You can work on multiple levels at the same time, perhaps even all four levels.

Keep working on yourself and remember they don't call it the leadership *journey* for nothing.

90. Self-Awareness, Self-Reflection

Have you ever noticed how some people are really good at understanding themselves? And that they have a vision that is clear and empowering; they know their strengths, but just as importantly, they know their weaknesses.

The latter point is important, especially when developing a team, since if you know your team's or organization's blind spots, you can fill those. You will also know where to focus your energy, or where you need to learn new soft or hard skills if you're lacking or downright missing them.

So, here's a brief exercise to help you. Put this into your digital note-taker app, your journal, or just write it on post-it notes. Think about it, but don't overthink it. Just start writing. You can edit it after.

- What are you most proud of (in terms of accomplishments or life events) in the last 365 days?

- What have been your greatest challenges? Have you overcome them? How have you overcome them?

- What are your top three learnings from the past year?

- If you had to thank people for the person you are today, who would they be? Write their names down. Might be a good idea to thank them in person or send them a message as well. I'm sure they would love to hear the impact they had on you.

- What is your theme for next year (or this year, if it's early in the year when you're writing these out)? It could be words, a phrase, a drawing, or a picture.

Reflection is a great source of continuous learning about yourself. It's free and not many leaders do it. Use it as a tool.

91. Vision is a Lot More Than Words

What is your vision for the future? If you do not know the answer, then how do you know where you're going?

Now, don't worry. Many people don't know their vision. Even the company you own or work for may have a cloudy or undefined vision. Your vision for the future must align with your values.

If you want to be the best hands-on surgeon in the world, but you want to work from a beach and soak up the sun every day, those aspects of your vision are probably mis-matched. Same for the uber-driven executive whose vision is to be the best dad and husband in the world, yet works until 10:00 p.m. every night and misses supper and bedtime with the kids.

My vision and values are centred on being the best dad, best leader, and best mentor I can be, while continuously learning and finding time every day for exercise and meditation.

Control of my time, and freedom are also vital to my work and life. It took me many years to put it all together, and I am still adding to this vision, but having a purpose certainly helps align my values, which centre around: spending quality time with family (especially my kids), personal development, exercise routines, work habits, eating habits, and learning. Also, it's easier to say no to people or things that are not aligned with my vision.

Keep in mind that the most important thing for you to remember is to not simply write your vision down. But to live it. Ken Blanchard and Jesse Lyn Stoner so aptly remind us of this in *Full Steam Ahead! Unleash the Power of Vision in Your Company and Your Life.*

> *"Vision is a lot more than putting a plaque on the wall. A real vision is lived, not framed."*[xx]

I hope this gets you thinking about what you want your vision of the future to be. And then align that with your values.

It's a daily, weekly, monthly, yearly process.

The crucial thing for you is to start living an aligned life as soon as possible.

92. Your Idea of Failure Reflects on You

Some people are so focused on failure, they are afraid to even try.

They are the *"yeah, but"* people. Always looking for a reason to put you, your idea, or themselves down. "That won't work" they say to every new idea they hear. If you've read this far, and are one of those people, and recognize that in yourself— please change.

You can't be a great future leader with that mindset. But if you recognize this and can give it a name, that's a big step.

If you see yourself in this mindset, you have to spin it. Be open-minded. Be more optimistic rather than less optimistic.

Listen even more than you judge.

Catch yourself when you become the *"that won't work"* person and be supportive.

And yes, it's okay to provide words of caution, just do it mindfully.

93. The Airport Test

Search for "the airport test" on Google and you'll get about 642 million search results. The airport test became a valuable tool in my interview arsenal after I kept reading about it in many leadership books.

What's the airport test, you're wondering?

In addition to looking for the qualifications and skills that align with the role they are hiring for, the hiring manager should ask themselves: "Would I want to be stuck in an airport with this person?"

Picture you and the candidate (or you, the candidate, and some of your team members) travelling to a conference, with a three-hour layover in Chicago.

Would there be dead silence, would you both just be cracking away at your emails, or would you be able to have some solid, interesting, and potentially fun(ny) conversations with this individual?

Now, some may say this is hard to know coming out of an interview. But if you feel the candidate was not being their true self, or was guarded in answering all the questions, or too polished in an inauthentic way, would you hire that person?

Granted, you might need a second or third interview to get to know them better, but if you have a shadow of a doubt about their authenticity in that interview, you likely already know whether or not you should hire them.

Also, let me add: this isn't just a social contest. They absolutely *need* to have the relevant hard and soft skills, qualifications, and experience for the role. The airport test takes it just a bit further than that.

For the amount of time you'll be spending with them, you want to like and get along with this person. Some people hate small talk, and that's okay. But an airport is usually a great place to get to know your team members.

And if you've ever had plane delays or airport layovers, you'll know they can get quite tiresome and sometimes boring. So, enjoying the time you have with an employee can make the time pass faster, and at the same time, you get to know them on a more personal level.

The next time you're interviewing a potential hire, in your mind, make sure you ask yourself: "would I want to spend time with this person while I'm stuck in an airport?" Works every time.

94. Best Definition of Being a Leader

Every person in a position of power or authority— or anyone who has a team under them—believes they are a good, if not a great, leader and this is because self-awareness is a challenge for many people. But there is a terrific definition of leadership that is as humbling as it is inspiring. And if this does not get your heart going and get you excited about developing and inspiring others, I'm not sure what will.

Going back to what John Quincy Adams said:

"If your actions inspire others to dream more, learn more, do more, and become more, you are a leader."

Be those words.

Now, be honest with yourself. Do you inspire this in your team? If you do, kudos. If you don't, what will you change today? What actions or communication pattern will you change? Chart out a plan to ensure you inspire your team to be more and be there to push and support them.

95. Golden Interview Question to Ask

If ever you're lucky enough to be in an interview where the owner or president is in the same room as another exec (likely someone from HR) there's a good way learn if employees can be open and honest with their boss in the room; if they can't, that says a lot about the organization.

Because it's one thing for the company to *talk about* placing a high value on being open and transparent before you get there. It's another thing to live and breathe those principles daily.

Every company claims to have great values and respect for employees and partners. Only a few of them follow through on those claims.

Here's an example: I was once in an interview with a president and three of his direct reports. So, during my interview, I asked the three direct reports, with the president in the room: "What do you love about coming to work, and what is the one thing you would change?" I have since asked this anytime direct reports are in the same interview with the head honcho. I am looking for honesty and transparency, seeing if they are unafraid to tell the truth about what the company or, potentially, their leadership team, needs to do better.

I got two answers that were very polished and one that was very honest in a refreshing and respectful way. I made sure to see how the President reacted. He did not seem perturbed in the least. Kudos to that individual for being honest.

It shows immense confidence to be respectfully critical and it shows that people know the issues, but they want your help in fixing them.

However, two out of the three direct reports were unwilling or afraid to be honest. That also spoke volumes to me.

96. Caring is Not a Weakness

Whether it's right or wrong, the workplace hasn't always been a welcoming and caring place for everyone.

Typically, the top brass demands things from their "soldiers" and often in commanding and dominating ways. In the last 30 years or so, that has certainly begun to change, but over the next 30 years and beyond we need to see a complete shift.

Caring about your employees should be a pre-requisite for any current and future leader. But this cannot simply be lip service; it can't be about simply saying you care but acting very differently

To care for your employees is to treat them with respect, and not just on Fridays, but every single day; and not just when things are good, but especially when the waves come in; not just when results are better than expected, but when you hit turbulence.

To truly care for your employees means you are empathetic to their needs and wants, and communication is free flowing. To care for your employees means you care about their development, even if that means they may outgrow the role you have for them. If you care for your employees, they will care about you, the organization, and its values. And that will likely result in excellent performance.

As quoted in *Leadership from The Inside Out*, Marilyn Carlson Nelson, one of Fortune Magazine's 50 most powerful Women in Business, said: *"Employees who feel that their management cares about them as a person, in return care about the organization in which they work. And isn't that the key to a successful enterprise?"*[xxi]

Yes, it certainly is. Caring for your employees may actually be the most overlooked element of success for most companies.

97. Your Word is Your Bond

Social media giant Gary Vaynerchuk often says, "Your Word is Your Bond," and I absolutely love it! I once reported to a leader who I admired and respected, except for one thing – when he said he would do something, I didn't often believe it.

For example, he'd say, "let's meet this week." But when I asked for times to meet, my email went unanswered. When trying to set up a meeting with vendors, he said he would let me know a time by the afternoon. After two or three follow-ups, I finally got a time... three days later.

Getting sign-offs on projects took weeks and not days. After my plan was approved and given the green light, it took months of make-work (you know, the kind of work where you are asked for small details that have been reviewed five times already) before the investment followed.

You see, his word wasn't his bond. And it was not intentional. Not at all. But if there is a checklist of factors on which you need to trust your boss and vice versa, their word ranks high up on that list.

This is fairly simple to do at times, but very hard to carry out consistently: if you say you'll do something, follow through, or provide an update or reason for why it wasn't done.

98. Why We Fear Change

Businesses today have never enjoyed so many possibilities and opportunities to thrive, yet this is also the most difficult of times to survive.

There is a lot of competition and there are fewer barriers to entering most businesses and industries.

Plus, many innovators and other people with great minds are joining start-ups or launching their own businesses rather than looking for employment at traditional companies.

What's more, one overwhelming issue in all this can, if ignored, guarantee failure for many businesses before they even start.

What is that, you ask? Simple: the fear of change, and the refusal to accept the need to adapt.

In *Leadership from The Inside Out*, Kevin Cashman says that:

> *"We fear it (change) because change always involved both creation and destruction. As something new is created, something old is destroyed. The bud is destroyed as the flower blooms. The chrysalis is destroyed as the butterfly ascends. Our hesitation comes as we face the prospect of replacing the familiar with the unknown."*[xxii]

Have you ever lost your job? Have you ever gone through a break-up? Have you lost something or someone and thought you would never recover? These are generally drastic events that *force* change upon you. And if you look back at any events that forced you to change, I'm pretty certain you came out of it better, or at least—in the case of losing somebody—grew as a person to levels you didn't think you could reach.

You found inner strength, and while you may not have embraced change at that time, you eventually had to accept it so you could move on.

So, why do we fight it for so long sometimes? Why do we fight the company's decision for a new Enterprise Resource Planning (ERP) system, knowing it'll be better for the company in the long run, but we just don't want to learn a new technology?

Why do we fight the new management team coming in, knowing they have tons of vital experience? Why do we hate changing jobs, even though we have grown stagnant and stressed in our current role?

The quicker you learn to adapt to change, the quicker success will follow you. Adaptability is a great currency. Be sure to cultivate lots of it during this insanely fast-paced and changing world we live in today.

99. The Chart That Explains It All

Okay. So maybe this doesn't explain it *all*. But it's an insightful comparison between a boss and a leader. It's also interesting if you see yourself in either of these lists and can identify what changes you might want to make in the next 365 days.

Read this chart below and put a checkmark beside or highlight the trait that most closely defines you on each line: And don't be too hard on yourself if you find yourself in the "boss" column for a couple of these juxtapositions, or for most of them, for that matter. Just try to work yourself out of them. Especially at the beginning of your career. Being a leader requires constant learning to understand people, team, accountability, character, and how they each work together to inspire and drive performance to the next level. But when in doubt, choose the characteristics of a leader over a boss.

Are You a Boss or a Leader?

BOSS:	LEADER:
Dictatorial approach	*Consultative, learning
Issues orders	*Collaborates, seeks input
Very critical of others	*Supportive, encouraging
Puts themselves first	*Considerate of employees
Always blames others	*Takes responsibility
Close-minded	*Open-minded, receptive
Condescending	*Values, inspires others
Doesn't listen	*Listens, values opinions

---

100. Adjust The Sails!

"The pessimist complains about the wind. The optimist expects it to change. The leader adjusts the sails."
—John Maxwell

Yesterday may have been a tough one. Today may be filled with unexpected challenges. But tomorrow will improve.

Sometimes, you need to remain calm, and if your plan or tactic is not working, or your strategy is not sinking in with the team, adjust.

Find out what's not working and why it's not working and then go about setting your sail forward.

Become a leader worth following.

101. 12 Months to Improve Your Weakness

If there was one thing you knew was important to gain for your career to vault ahead, what would it be?

It could be a category or function (like math or finance, like writing or communication) or it could be something like public speaking or being nicer to people. Whatever you think will move that needle and level you up, write it down.

Now, what if you spent the next 12 months focussing on that topic? Read all the books and articles that can help you, practice with your spouse, friends, co-workers, or family members, follow and engage with 10 social media accounts on this topic, find the five best podcasts on this, and start improving.

If self-improving and overcoming this weakness is important for your career development and growth, wouldn't it be wise to spend some time gaining knowledge in it, and closing the gap? The next level is within reach sooner than you think.

So, you should now write down what this self-improvement opportunity is, and then spend the next 12 months chasing that knowledge and expertise.

102. Should Trust Be Earned or Given?

I give trust. I give it with open arms. Always.

Have I been burned at times? Yes, but I can count those times on one hand. That is just the way I am. I don't judge, I treat people fairly, and I am open and honest.

When I meet someone, or someone comes to work for me, I always like them at first and try to see the good in them. Sure, I get along easier with some personalities than others, but who am I to judge them in any negative way? That's just the way I'm wired.

But I know there are many people and leaders out there who believe in the "trust must be earned" motto. So essentially, you close off people or don't give them the benefit of the doubt until they prove their worth. And where is that bar set? How does one get into that trust circle? Is it after 12 months of results? Is it after five large projects? Is it after five years of service? Is it after having a few nightcaps with them and having each of you open up? Does that person or your employee know you don't trust them yet?

I feel that's a backwards way to lead.

Hey, I know many people who have been burned in relationships and, perhaps understandably, they don't want to trust openly again. I can understand that in some ways on a personal level.

But if you are a leader and you have a team and your belief is that they have to claw and earn your trust, I feel that is not being a mindful leader, as you are somehow expecting them to fail. Wouldn't your employees perform better knowing they can trust you, and that you trust them?

Have you ever worked for someone or had a coach who you kind of felt didn't trust you? It's not a great feeling, because then you are on edge and always trying to impress them to get that feeling of trust, but you are so tense it actually hampers your work (or, in sports, your game).

Now, while I trust openly and give it to all employees, if that trust is betrayed, there is very little anyone can do to get back to any type of trust level. The bridge may be permanently burned. But I would rather serve the 98% of my past, current, and future teams, and risk that 2%, than be closed to the idea of trusting people openly.

You can choose to either trust openly or require people to earn it. Which camp would you prefer your boss was in? After answering that question, you might come to an easy conclusion on how best to lead. But it's your choice.

103. 15 Minutes to Make Your Team Smile

Promise you'll read this and immediately action it? Okay. Deal. Then read on.

Take the next 15 minutes right now and thank *every* member of your team (if you don't have a team, send it to your closest partners and vendors. You can even do this for your own family). Make it a team email or chat message, so they all can see it. Include your boss if you want so he or she sees the tremendous value your team brings to the company.

Say something like: *Grateful time! Just wanted to say a big thank you to all of you. This week you all dove in like crazy! I appreciate it.*

And then, name by name, list all the great things they've done in the last week (or month) and thank them for it—say "thank you, first name."

Now put this book down and make your team smile. I bet you'll feel better too!

104. The Goal of a Performance Review

I once had a performance review with my boss that pretty much went as expected, save for one piece. I left feeling unmotivated.

Now, the goal of a performance review *should be* to gauge how the last year or quarter went, and it should identify some helpful areas for improvement.

It should also encourage and motivate your employee for the next year (or quarter) ahead. Some also may serve as a warning, or last chance for employees with little future in the company.

Well, the year in question, I met all my goals. At this company, employees also rated their own performance, on a scale of 1-5. Both me and my boss gave me the same grade—which translated to "above expectations."

I figured that meant it was at least a pretty good year.

But my boss said something no one else has ever said to me in my entire career: *"Johnny, for the salary we pay you, we expect even more. You're one of our highest-paid employees."*

If he felt that was a way to light a fire under me, he was mistaken. It did the opposite. I wanted to say something like:

"Well, boss, you pay me that amount because that's what the market dictates." Or

"No one forced you into this agreement when I was hired." Or even

"Maybe you should pay your employees more," (as the company was notorious for underpaying most employees).

But I didn't. I sat there with little reaction because I knew it would not help. Clearly, he did not see the value I was bringing, and he didn't know why he paid me more than others. My team and I surpassed our goals and KPIs, our department had the best culture in the company, and we had the lowest turnover rate. So, his comment caught me a bit off guard.

But I tell this story here to help you. Use your critical feedback or performance reviews as a point in time to level up with your employee(s), be open and honest with them, and end with a positive note or story, one that motivates the employee, and not one that makes the employee feel devalued, as was the case when my boss threw the money I made in my face, almost as an insult.

In *Good People,* author Anthony Tjan writes,

> *"Leaders are committed to improving everyone around them just as much as they are committed to improving themselves.*
> *They feel a duty to serve others by inspiring and shaping them to become the best, fullest version of themselves. The leaders and people who do this don't create followers, they create more leaders."*[xxiii]

Choose your words and plan wisely as you enter a performance review. The goal is to elevate your employees and make them better. Simply put: create more leaders.

105. People Define Your Leadership Ability

It's not the years of experience you have that makes you a solid leader. It's not the title you have that makes people want to work with you. Not even a leadership self-assessment can really determine if you are a great manager. No. Only your people can do that.

As Clint Pulver says in his book, *I Love It Here: How Great Leaders Create Organizations Their People Never Want to Leave:*

> *"Your title might make you a supervisor but your people will decide if you're a mentor."*[xxiv]

The fundamentals of being a good leader are not very complicated: communicate well and often, truly care for your people, mentor, coach, and teach them, show respect (to your employees, colleagues, bosses, vendors, etc.) even during tough times, provide feedback when your employees do things right and wrong, and drive results.

The difference between a good leader and a great leader, is that a great leader does all these things all the time, or at least more often than not.

But never use your title as a way to demand leadership. Quality leadership is determined by the people you lead.

Last Word

In a piece of beautiful writing on the topic of human capital, I will let famed leadership guru Ken Blanchard tell this story:

> *"As for me, I'm still working on my vision of moving from success to significance. I've discovered that as we move full steam ahead toward our vision, our vision expands the closer we come to it. My vision has expanded to include my community. I've realized that on this planet, we are all part of one community, and we all need to assume responsibility for creating a shared vision."*[xxv]

And Blanchard sums it up in Insta-shareable point form:[xxvi]

- *When you're ready to move from Success to Significance, it's time to think about giving back to the community*

- *The vision is about more than just you*

- *We're all in this world together*

Moving from *Success* to *Significance*. It's a great line. And we are all on different leadership journeys, different life adventures.

There will be ups and there will be downs. Some people are just beginning, and others are entrenched in their journeys.

And I wrote this book to give back. I saw too much old-school thinking early in my career; managers— thankfully, they were not mine — who did not appreciate their employees, didn't mentor or coach them, heaped blame upon them, and didn't have their backs. My team, past and present, is my family. They always will be.

So, this book is a thank you to all the great bosses I've had along the way (you know who you are), the great authors and motivators who inspired me, and all my fantastic team members who allowed me to grow, and continue to grow, into the leader I want and need to become.

Being a parent has also evolved my leadership, and I've grown into patience while still pushing for the best my team can give me.

And I wrote this book to serve you, the people I am grateful are reading the words on these pages, and also the people (current and future leaders) I am so thankful want to buy in to a new type of leadership, one that always respects people, seeks out the good, and remains positive, even during challenging times. This includes managers who want to become leaders and coaches that their employees and team members love to work for and see succeed; task-oriented directors or VPs who want to level-up to people-oriented mentors; presidents and owners who seek profitability, but also a better culture, one centred on people and profits together, more empowerment without blame, and a reduction in turnover.

You are all the present and the future. Success to Significance. Let's walk together on this journey.

Let's Chat!

Continue your leadership journey and connect personally with Johnny at:

Instagram: @Russo_Johnny
Facebook:
https://www.facebook.com/johnnyrusso19
TikTok: https://www.tiktok.com/@russo_johnny
LinkedIn:
https://www.linkedin.com/in/johnnyrusso/
Twitter: @Russojohnny
Personal Website: http://www.johnnyrusso.com/
Blog: http://www.johnnyrusso.com/blog/
Book Website:
www.themindfulleaderplaybook.com/

You can also message Johnny at any of the above channels for speaking engagements.

Acknowledgements

This book was written over a couple of years. I began writing it on flights, when I had the least number of distractions.

I also started writing it before I became a dad. I was probably halfway through writing many concepts you find on these pages when my leadership journey became even more fulfilled – I became Daddy to someone. Luca was first, followed by Siena. People don't often think of parents as leaders, but the good ones are every... single... day!

Writing this book has been a journey. It was not filled with anguish but filled with contentment that I could help inspire just one person, be it a former team member, a former colleague, or a complete stranger embarking on, or in the middle of, their leadership journey. I hope I accomplished that goal.

A major part of being a good leader is surrounding yourself with great people. I think I did that.

To my leadership coach, Colin Holbrow, thank you for your help in self-reflection, and your kind words along the way. Thank you for also making the introduction to Susan Crossman, my book editor who walked a former journalist through this complex publishing process to get you the book you are physically holding or reading digitally. Your wise recommendations were truly appreciated. And thank you for the intro to Manor House Publishing. Mike Davie and the team at Manor House have been great to work with. I am so thankful they did all the (publishing) heavy lifting to get this book ready for reading. I am indebted to you guys.

Thank you to Dominic Ruggeri for the amazing website design. You're a friend, a brother, and so much more.

To my former and current leaders: this book has your name written all over it. You empowered me to become the leader I am, and I have a long way to go, but I will never forget what you did and continue to do for me. You inspire me. In order of when I met you: Peter MacKie, Jacques Duguay, Don Belanger, Tomas Schmidt, Francois de Repentigny, Stephen White, Michel Bitton, Olivia Bitton, Georgia Genovezos, John Gunn, Sandra Broccoli, Anne-Hélène Hars, Greg Moreau, Stephanie Bleau, David Lui, Rick White, PJ Czank, Kerry Munro, John Koryl, Jacquie Marvell-Potts, Daniel Lieberman, Martin Lieberman, the Lieberman family and Steven Nadler. There were others to be sure, but you impacted my career in ways you may never know. So, this is a thank you to you all.

To my family: my parents, Josee and Leo, who continue to give and give and give and show compassion and love for their family. I lead the way you raised me. Thank you.

To my grandparents watching from above, Nonna and Nonno, ti amo sempre.

To my brothers, Joe and Anthony, and their wonderful wives and kids (my beautiful nephews): caring is at the centre of this new breed of leadership I hope to help spread, and as your little brother, you always made time for me, and I was never too young to be around you or your friends growing up. Thank you.

To Teresa and Carmine, you helped as I watched you hold high-level corporate positions while raising four beautiful daughters. You showed how you can balance career, family life, and fun. Thank you.

To Jasmine: they say life is a journey with problems to solve and lessons to learn but most of all, experiences to enjoy. We've enjoyed so many beautiful moments…and thank you for your patience as this book was being written. You're a fantastic Mom to Luca and Siena. Thank you.

To my kids, Luca and Siena: your hugs warm my heart, your kisses make me wish for more - and nighttime cuddles while reading is my favourite time of day. I love you more than you may ever know. You are my life. When people ask what I do, or who I am, I have the same answer. I am a dad, first and foremost. Thank you.

To my readers: thank you for picking up this book. I am forever grateful. Tony Robbins says, *"the only impossible journey is the one you never begin."*

I hope you begin to see leadership in a different way. We're counting on you. And if you're already a great leader, and doing many of these things, kudos to you. We need more of you.

Please connect with me on the social channels on page 179 or be sure to say hi if we're ever at the same event or conference. It would be my pleasure to connect.

About the Author

Johnny Russo is a seasoned business leader who has managed countless teams over the course of a career that has harnessed the concept of mindful leadership to the success of the people he has been privileged to lead.

He has worked for large public companies, medium sized-private companies, and family-owned and run businesses. Regardless of the size of the company or teams, his leadership—and how he brings a team together—remains focused on empowering his people to:

- continuously learn and adapt

- be unafraid to make mistakes, and

- be willing to swing for the fences in order to succeed

Over his career, Johnny has had the chance to work with some great leaders and managers, but he's also seen examples of how *not to* manage and lead a team.

Having read more than 100 leadership books since his career began, he noticed that many of them were fantastic reads, but they were routinely aimed at the top ranks, the C-suite, or the VP level and above. Most were written by consultants or retired leaders.

Johnny decided to write a leadership playbook while he's in the day-to-day trenches of corporate life in order to assist:

- **new managers** to lead a successful team

- **current managers** to level up their leadership, and

- **successful leaders** to take on a more mindful leadership practice

Johnny is determined to help lead via respect, values, inspiration, and care, and he issues a call to action for people to get behind *the* new age of leadership, one that respects and encourages employees—at last.

Johnny believes mindful leadership practices will lead to happier employees, and a better world.

To bring Johnny's insights into your day-to-day world you can contact him at: johnnyrusso19@gmail.com

References

---

[i] Ray Dalio, *Principles: Life and Work (New York: Simon and Schuster, 2017)* 348.

[ii] Dalio, *Principles*, 388.

[iii] Ray Dalio, "Principles," Nepabox, http://nepabox.com/story/principles-life-work/

[iv] Kevin Cashman *Leadership from the Inside Out: Becoming a Leader for Life*, (San Francisco, CA: Berrett-Koehler, Second Edition, 2008) 108.

[v] Dalio, *Principle*, 91.

[vi] Jack Canfield, *The Success Principles*: *How to Get from Where You Are to Where You Want to Be* (New York: William Morrow, 2004) 195.

[vii] Canfield, *The Success Principles*, 195.

[viii] Judy Machado-Duque, *Life Purpose Playbook: The Ultimate Guide to Goal Setting and Daily Planning* (Scotts Valley, CA: CreateSpace, 2015) 14, 15, and 17.

[ix] Anthony Tjan, *Good People: The Only Leadership Decision That Really Matters*, New York: Portfolio Penguin, 2017), 18.

[x] Peter Gruber, *Tell to Win: Connect, Persuade, and Triumph with the Hidden Power of Story,* (New York: Crown Business, 2011) 18-19.

[xi] Dalio, Principles, 349.

[xii] Tjan, *Good People*, 88.

[xiii] Chuck Salter, FastCompany.com, "Failure Doesn't Suck," www.fastcompany.com/59549/failure-doesnt-suck

[xiv] Ken Blanchard and Garry Ridge, *Helping People Win at Work: A Business Philosophy Called "Don't Mark My Paper, Help Me Get an A,"* (Upper Saddle River, NJ: Polvera Publishing, 2009), 122.

[xv] Blanchard and Ridge, *Helping People Win at Work*, 123.

[xvi] Marshall Goldsmith, *Triggers: Creating Behavior That Lasts—Becoming the Person You Want to Be,* (Sydney, Currency Press, 2015), 86.

[xvii] Ken Blanchard, Thad Lacinak, Chuck Tompkins, and Jim Ballard, *Whale Done: The Power of Positive Relationships,* (New York: The Free Press, 2002).
[xviii] James H. Amos, Amazon.ca, https://www.amazon.com/Full-Steam-Ahead-Unleash-Vision/dp/1576753069#:~:text=%E2%80%9CA%20clear%20vision%20gives%20an,%E2%80%94James%20H.
[xix] Blanchard and Ridge, *Helping People Win at Work,* 137.
[xx] Ken Blanchard and Jesse Lyn Stoner, *Full Steam Ahead Unleash the Power of Vision in Your Company and Your Life,* (San Francisco, CA: Berrett-Koehler, 2011), 119.
[xxi] Cashman, *Leadership from The Inside Out, 114*
[xxii] Cashman, *Leadership from The Inside Out,* 132.
[xxiii] Tjan, *Good People,* 4.
[xxiv] Clint Pulver, *I Love It Here: How Great Leaders Create Organizations Their People Never Want to Leave.*
[xxv] Blanchard and Stoner, *Full Steam Ahead, 160.*
[xxvi] Blanchard and Stoner, *Full Steam Ahead*), 157.

Manor House Publishing Inc.
www.manor-house-publishing.com
905-648-4797

Manor House Publishing Inc.
www.manor-house-publishing.com
905-648-4797

Manor House Publishing Inc.
www.manor-house-publishing.com
905-648-4797

Manor House Publishing Inc.
www.manor-house-publishing.com
905-648-4797

Manor House Publishing Inc.
www.manor-house-publishing.com
905-648-4797

www.ingramcontent.com/pod-product-compliance
Lightning Source LLC
Chambersburg PA
CBHW071216210326
41597CB00016B/1841